Law E

CW00972422

SCOTTISH
ADMINISTRATIVE LAW

Law Essentials

SCOTTISH ADMINISTRATIVE LAW

Jean McFadden, M.A., LL.B.

Senior Lecturer in Law, University of Strathclyde and former leader of Glasgow City Council

and

Dale McFadzean, B.A.(Hons). F.H.E.A.

Lecturer in Law, University of Paisley

DUNDEE UNIVERSITY PRESS
2006

First published in Great Britain in 2006 by
Dundee University Press
University of Dundee
Dundee DD1 4HN

www.dundee.ac.uk/dup

ISBN 1–84586–013–6
EAN 978–1–84586–013–4

No natural forests were destroyed to make this product;
only farmed timber was used and replanted.

British Library Cataloguing-in-Publication Data
A catalogue record for this book is available on request from the British Library

Typeset by Waverley Typesetters, Fakenham, Norfolk
Printed and bound by Bell & Bain Ltd, Glasgow

CONTENTS

		Page
Table of Cases		vii
Table of Statutes		xi
1	Introduction	1
2	Doctrines of the Constitution	5
3	Structure of Government in the UK	19
4	Subordinate Legislation	25
5	The *Ultra Vires* Doctrine	37
6	Judicial Review	47
7	Natural Justice	65
8	Ombudsmen	77
9	Tribunals and Inquiries	89
Index		103

TABLE OF CASES

Page

A (A Mental Patient) *v* Scottish Ministers 2000 SLT 873 ....32, 35
Associated Provincial Picture Houses Ltd *v* Wednesbury Corporation
   [1948] 1 KB 223 ....37, 45, 56, 57, 58, 63
Attorney-General *v* Crayford Urban District Council [1962] Ch 575 40
— *v* Great Eastern Railway Co (1880) L.R. 5 App Cas 473 .... 39, 40, 46
— *v* Wilts United Dairies (1922) 38 TLR 781 ....26, 35, 37, 45
Attorney-General of Hong Kong *v* Ng [1983] 2 AC 629 72
Ayr Harbour Trustees *v* Oswald (1883) LR 8 App Cas 623 56

Baker *v* Glasgow District Council 1981 SC 258 61
Black *v* Tennant (1899) 49
Bradford *v* McLeod 1986 SLT 244 67
Brechin Golf and Squash Club *v* Angus District Licensing Board 1993 SLT 547 ....72, 75
British Oxygen Co *v* South-West Scotland Electricity Board [1956] 1 WLR 1069 60
Brown *v* Hamilton District Council 1983 SC (HL) 1 61

Chertsey Urban District Council *v* Mixnam's Properties Ltd [1964] 2 WLR 1210 54
Chester *v* Bateson [1920] 1 KB 829 ....27, 35, 38, 45
Cooper *v* Wandsworth Board (1863) 14 CB NS 180 69
— *v* Wilson [1937] 2 KB 309 67
Council of Civil Service Unions *v* Minister for Civil Service
   [1985] AC 374 .... 51, 56, 57, 63, 73
Crédit Suisse *v* Allerdale Borough Council [1996] 3 WLR 894 41
— *v* Waltham Forest London Borough Council [1996] 3 WLR 943 42

D & J Nicol *v* Dundee Harbour Trustees [1915] AC 550 ....39, 49
Darney *v* Calder District Council (1904) 12 SLT 546 60
Don Brothers, Buist & Co Ltd *v* Scottish National Insurance Commissioners
   1913 SC 607 52

Ellen Street Estates Ltd *v* Minister of Health [1934] 1 KB 590 ....12, 17
Eldon Garages Ltd *v* Kingston-upon-Hull County Borough Council [1974] 1 WLR 276 ... 59
Entick *v* Carrington (1765) 2 Wils KB 275 1
Errington *v* Wilson 1995 SC 550 ....70, 74

Gaiman *v* National Association for Mental Health [1970] 3 WLR 42 65
Glasgow Rape Crisis Centre *v* Home Secretary 2000 SC 527 49
Graham *v* Glasgow Corporation 1936 SC 108 ....40, 61
Grand National Canal Co *v* Dimes (1852) 3 HL Cas 759 ....66, 74
Great Portland Estates *v* Westminster City Council [1984] 3 WLR 1035 44
Grunwick Processing Laboratories Ltd *v* ACAS [1978] AC 655 59
Gunstone *v* Scottish Women's Amateur Athletic Association 1987 SLT 611 50
Guthrie *v* Miller (1827) 5 S 711 ....47, 63

Hamilton *v* Secretary of State for Scotland 1972 SC 72 100
Hannam *v* Bradford City Council [1970] 1 WLR 937 67

Hazell *v* Hammersmith and Fulham Borough Council [1992] 2 AC 1 41
Hibernian Property Co *v* Secretary of State for the Environment (1973) 72 LGR 350........ 69
Home *v* Young (1846) 50
Houston *v* Kerr (1890)... 66

Innes *v* Royal Burgh of Kirkcaldy 1963 SLT 325 62

Jenkins *v* Robertson (1867) LR 1 Sc 117 50
Joobeen *v* University of Stirling 1995 SLT 120..48, 49

Lavender & Son *v* Minister for Housing and Local Government [1970] 1 WLR 1231......... 55
Lee *v* Secretary of State for Education and Science (1968) 66 LGR 211 59
Lithgow *v* Secretary of State for Scotland 1973 SC 1... 99
Local Government Board *v* Arlidge [1915] AC 120 98
London and Clydeside Estates *v* Aberdeen District Council [1980] 1 WLR 182 59

McColl *v* Strathclyde Regional Council 1983 SC 225 .... 41, 46, 51, 61, 63
McDonald *v* Burns 1940 SC 376 48
— *v* Lanarkshire Fire Brigade Joint Committee 1959 SC 141.. 65
McEldowney *v* Forde [1971] AC 632...38, 46
Macfarlane *v* Glasgow Licensing Board 1971 SLT (Sh Ct) 9 53
Magistrates of Buckhaven and Methil *v* Wemyss Coal Co 1932 SC 201............................. 62
Malloch *v* Aberdeen Corporation 1974 SLT 253..27, 35, 38, 46
Manchester (Ringway Airport) Compulsory Purchase Order, Re (1935) 68
Meek *v* Lothian Regional Council 1983 SLT 494... 61
Morgan Guaranty Trust Co of New York *v* Lothian Regional Council 1995 SC 151 .....41, 46
Moss Empires *v* Assessor for Glasgow 1917 SC (HL) 1 .... 47, 59, 63

Nahar *v* Strathclyde Regional Council 1986 SLT 570 62
Naik *v* University of Stirling 1994 SLT 449..48, 49

O'Reilly *v* Mackman [1983] 2 AC 237 48

Palmer *v* Inverness Hospitals Board 1963 SC 311 60
Pett *v* Greyhound Racing Association [1968] 2 WLR 1471 ....70, 74
Pickin *v* British Railways Board [1974] AC 765 ....12, 17
Poyser & Mills' Arbitration, Re [1963] 2 WLR 1309 95
Purdon *v* City of Glasgow Licensing Board 1989 SLT 201 ....71, 75

R *v* Amber Valley District Council, ex parte Jackson [1984] 3 All ER 501 68
— *v* Barnsley Metropolitan Borough Council, ex parte Hook [1976] 1 WLR 1052.......58, 67
— *v* Criminal Injuries Compensation Board, ex parte RJC [1978] Crim LR 220............... 55
— *v* Ealing London Borough Council, ex parte Times Newspapers (1986) 85 LGR 316 53
— *v* Higher Education Funding Council, ex parte Institute of Dental Surgery
   [1994] 1 WLR 242... 71
— *v* Kent Police Authority, ex parte Godden [1971] 2 QB 662 ....67, 74
— *v* Kirklees Metropolitan Borough Council (1988) 152 LG Rev 27 ....44, 46
— *v* Leicester City Justices, ex parte Barrow [1991] 2 QB 260 ....70, 75
— *v* Local Commissioner for Administration for the North and East Area of England,
   ex parte Bradford City Council [1979] QB 287 86
— *v* Ministry of Defence, ex parte Smith [1996] QB 517... 58
— *v* Port of London Authority, ex parte Kynoch [1919] 1 KB 176................................... 55

R *v* Secretary of State for the Home Department, ex parte Doody [1994] 1 AC 531 71
— *v* Secretary of State for Trade and Industry, ex parte Greenpeace Ltd
     [1998] Env LR 415.. 50
— *v* —, ex parte Vardy [1993] 1 CMLR 721 73
— *v* Secretary of State for Transport, ex parte Factortame (No 2) [1991] 1 AC 603........14, 17
— *v* Thames Magistrates' Court, ex parte Polemis [1974] 1 WLR 1371 69
R (Association of British Civilian Internees – Far Eastern Region) *v* Secretary of State
     for Defence [2003] QB 1397 58
Ridge *v* Baldwin [1964] AC 40..2, 65, 69, 74
Roberts *v* Hopwood [1925] AC 578 ....53, 58
Rossi *v* Edinburgh Corporation (1904) 12 SLT 435; (1903) 10 SLT 662........................54, 61

St Johnstone FC *v* Scottish Football Association 1965 SLT 171 48
Schmidt *v* Secretary of State for Home Affairs [1969] 2 Ch 149 72
Scottish Old People's Welfare Council, Petrs 1987 SLT 179 ....50, 63
Shetland Line *v* Secretary of State for Scotland 1996 SLT 653 60
Short *v* Poole Corporation [1926] Ch 66 57
Smith & Griffin *v* Lord Advocate 1950 SC 448 61
Strang *v* Stewart (1864).. 50
Stringer *v* Minister for Housing and Local Government [1971] 1 All ER 65....................... 56

Vine *v* National Dock Labour Board [1957] AC 488...27, 35, 39, 54

Watt *v* Lord Advocate 1979 SC 120 ....52, 53
West *v* Secretary of State for Scotland 1992 SC 385 .... 47, 48, 63
Wildridge *v* Anderson (1897) 5 SLT 206...66, 74
Wilson *v* IBA 1979 SC 351.. 50

X *v* Morgan Grampian Ltd [1991] 1 AC 1 ....14, 17

Zia *v* Secretary of State for the Home Department 1994 SLT 288 71

TABLE OF STATUTES

Page

1879	Ayr Harbour Act	56
1911	National Insurance Act	1
1916	New Ministries and Secretaries Act	37–38
1921	Tribunals of Inquiry (Evidence) Act	100
1922	Civil Authorities (Special Powers) (Northern Ireland) Act	38, 39
1931	Statute of Westminster	
	s 4	12
1946	Statutory Instruments Act	
	s 2(1)	30
1947	Crown Proceedings Act	11
	s 2	11
1956	Schools (Scotland) Act	38
1958	Tribunals and Inquiries Act	89, 95
1962	Education (Scotland) Act	38
	Town and Country Planning Act	56
1963	Betting, Gaming and Lotteries Act	53
	Sch 4	53
1964	Caravan Sites and Control of Development Act	54
1967	Parliamentary Commissioner for Administration Act	77, 78, 79, 80, 85, 87
	Sch 2	78
	Sch 3	79
1971	Sheriff Courts (Scotland) Act	10
	Town and Country Planning Act	44
1972	European Communities Act	13, 14, 17
	Local Government Act	
	s 111	41, 42
	Road Traffic Act	25
1973	Local Government (Scotland) Act	
	s 69	45, 46
	s 69(1)	41
	ss 201–204	34
1974	Health and Safety at Work etc Act	26
1975	House of Commons Disqualification Act	
	s 2	6
	Ministers of the Crown Act	20
1976	Local Government (Miscellaneous Provisions) Act	
	s 19	42
1980	Water (Scotland) Act	51
	s 6(1)	41, 51
1981	Supreme Court Act	10
1984	Mental Health (Scotland) Act	32, 33
1987	Abolition of Domestic Rates etc (Scotland) Act	13
1988	Local Government Finance Act	13
1991	Dangerous Dogs Act	13, 25
	s 2(4)	28

1992   Tribunals and Inquiries Act 90, 92, 93, 97, 101
            s 9 99
            s 10 95
1993   Judicial Pensions and Retirement Act 10
1994   Local Government etc (Scotland) Act 23
1997   Local Government (Contracts) Act 41–42
            s 6 42
1998   Government of Wales Act 21–22
            s 22 25
            Human Rights Act 2, 3, 13, 31, 57
            Northern Ireland Act
            s 5 25
            Scotland Act 10, 21, 22, 24, 31, 33
            s 28 .... 22, 24, 25, 31
            s 29 31
            s 29(2) 31
            s 30 26
            s 45 22
            s 91 82
            s 95 10
            Sch 4 .... 26, 31
            Sch 5 .... 22, 26, 31
            Sch 6 .... 24, 32, 35
            Sch 6, Pt 1 32
1999   Mental Health (Public Safety and Appeals) (Scotland) Act 32, 33
2002   Scottish Public Services Ombudsman Act 82, 84, 87
            s 5 84
            Sch 2 83
            Sch 2, Pt 1 83
            Sch 2, Pt 2 83
            Sch 4 83
2003   Local Government in Scotland Act 23, 24, 43, 45
2005   Constitutional Reform Act 6, 8, 16
            s 3 9

1 INTRODUCTION

Administrative law is one of the most interesting areas of public law and one which can potentially affect all of us. So what is it all about? A definition can make it sound quite dry and boring. For example: "Administrative law is the body of principles and rules governing the functions and powers of all the agencies of government, including government ministers, who are concerned with the application and administration of government policy." In real life, we are all affected by the work of "agencies of government". Most children in Scotland are educated in schools run by local councils; we all drink water provided by Scottish Water; and most of us use the National Health Service at some point in our lives. These are just a few of the administrative bodies that we take for granted. But what happens when an administrative body takes a decision or acts (or fails to act) in some way that affects one of us adversely? That is where administrative law comes into play. It can enable individuals who have been aggrieved by the activities of such bodies to seek redress and to enforce duties. Sometimes this will involve going to the Court of Session to seek what is called judicial review but, at other times, another body such as an ombudsman or a tribunal may provide the solution.

Administrative law has a long history – although it has not always been known by that name. As long ago as the 17th and 18th centuries, the courts were prepared to keep the powers of government in check. For example, in the case of *Entick v Carrington* (1765), the Home Secretary issued a general warrant which ordered King's Messengers to break into Entick's house and to seize his books and papers. Entick sued them as having acted unlawfully and the court decided that the Home Secretary's warrant was illegal because there was no Act of Parliament or other law which authorised it. Thus, a Government Minister was held not to be above the law. But the power and influence of the state remained comparatively small, as far as the individual citizen was concerned, until the mid-19th century when Parliament began to pass Public Health Acts and Factory Acts and other regulatory legislation, and all sorts of boards, inspectorates and commissions were set up to police their operations.

The 20th century saw a real expansion of welfare-related law. The Welfare State can probably be dated from the National Insurance Act of 1911 and it developed fairly rapidly during that century. The state is now involved in our lives from the cradle to the grave, ensuring that our births, marriages and deaths are registered, our children are educated, our old folk are provided with pensions and social services, and the unemployed with training and benefits. There are now far more occasions when the ordinary citizen can be seriously disadvantaged by the decisions of administrative bodies. However, administrative law did not keep pace with the development of administrative bodies, partly because of two World Wars where the need for decisive executive action was paramount. The judges also became bogged down in unnecessary distinctions as to whether decision-makers were acting in a judicial, executive or administrative capacity – to the detriment of individuals who had been dealt with in an administrative capacity.

But from the 1960s on, administrative law became reinvigorated and the judges began to flex their muscles again and reject the ideas that the powers of government agencies and Ministers should not be held in check and that decisions had to be made in a judicial capacity if the rules of natural justice were to apply. The turning point was the case of *Ridge v Baldwin* (1964) where the Chief Constable of Brighton was dismissed from his office without notice and without an opportunity to put his case. His appeal eventually reached the House of Lords, the highest court of appeal in the land. Lord Reid gave the leading judgment and made it clear that natural justice and the right to a hearing apply universally. This case gave a real boost to the development of administrative law and since then the judges have been expanding the boundaries of natural justice or "fairness" to include the enforcement of a person's legitimate expectations, the duty to give reasons for actions and decisions, and the need for proportionality.

Let's fast-forward to the closing years of the 20th century and the dawn of the 21st. In 1998 the Human Rights Act was passed which incorporated the provisions of the European Convention on Human Rights into UK law, allowing individuals to enforce their rights in the British courts. Judges have enhanced powers and can now declare an act of a public authority to be incompatible with the Human Rights Act. The year 2001 saw the terrorist attack on the Twin Towers in New York and since then the UK Parliament has passed anti-terrorist legislation which can drastically curtail people's individual rights and freedoms. The courts have been asked to rule on these curtailments on many occasions. So the boundaries of administrative law are continually expanding and it has become an even more powerful tool in protecting human rights.

Although much of administrative law is UK-wide, there are aspects of it which are distinctively Scottish. The rules as to who can apply for judicial review in the Scottish courts differ from the rules in England and Wales. In Scotland, unlike in England and Wales, there does not have to be an element of public law involved in an action to enable a successful application for judicial review. There have been cases where decisions of the Scottish Football Association and even the Roman Catholic Church have been successfully challenged. There is also a distinctive public sector ombudsman in Scotland. And now, of course, we have our own Scottish Parliament. The Acts of the Scottish Parliament, unlike Acts of the UK Parliament, are not supreme and their validity can be reviewed by the courts. They must also be in accordance with the Human Rights Act 1998, as must the acts and decisions of the Scottish Executive.

It is the Scottish dimension which makes this book by Dale McFadzean so valuable. There is no up-to-date Scottish textbook on administrative law. English textbooks, while containing much interesting and relevant case law, rarely give even so much as a nod in the direction of Scots law. Having mastered the basics of Scots administrative law by reading this book, readers can then turn to the English textbooks (some of which run to over a thousand pages), confident as to what is relevant to Scotland and what is not.

2 DOCTRINES OF THE CONSTITUTION

Constitutional law and administrative law are inextricably linked and in order fully to understand the workings of contemporary administrative law, the reader must also be aware of the fundamental doctrines of the British constitution. These doctrines frame and lend explanatory significance to the concepts contained within administrative law. Therefore, the purpose of this chapter is to give the reader an overview and a reminder of the key doctrines of the UK constitution.

SEPARATION OF POWERS

The classic exposition of the separation of powers is that of Montesquieu:

> "When the legislative and executive powers are united in the same person, or in the same body of magistrates, there can be no liberty ... Again, there is no liberty if the power of judging is not separated from the legislative and executive. If it were joined with the legislative, the life and liberty of the subject would be exposed to arbitrary control; for the judge would then be the legislator. If it were joined to the executive power, the judge might behave with violence and oppression. There would be an end to everything, if the same man, or the same body, whether of the nobles or of the people, were to exercise those three powers, that of enacting laws, that of executing public affairs, and that of trying crimes or individual causes." (*The Spirit of the Laws* (1748))

The doctrine of the separation of powers recognises three separate organs of government, namely the legislature, the executive and the judiciary. In the UK, the legislature is represented by the UK Parliament and devolved institutions, the executive by Ministers and the various organs of government, and the judiciary by judges applying the law. Each organ should be vested with one main function of government only and should not interfere with the functions of another. Yet it is debatable to what extent this separation truly exists in the UK.

Membership overlap

Legislature and executive
A complete separation of powers would mean that there should be no Ministers in Parliament; but by convention UK Government Ministers should be members either of the House of Commons or of the House of

Lords. This in turn makes them accountable and responsible to Parliament. There is, however, a statutory limit placed upon the number of Ministers who may sit and vote as members of the House of Commons. That number is currently limited to 95 Ministers by virtue of s 2 of the House of Commons Disqualification Act 1975. That same Act disqualifies many categories of office-holders from membership of the House of Commons, such as civil servants, police and members of the armed forces. Many civil servants, and the police, are also forbidden to take part in political activities, therefore the separation of the legislature and the executive is quite strict and it is only Ministers who hold a dual role. The same can be said of the devolved institutions within the UK.

Judiciary and legislature

There is membership overlap in the House of Lords, since the Lord Chancellor and the Law Lords (for the time being, until the provisions of the Constitutional Reform Act 2005 come fully into force) are judges and members of the legislature. But all other full-time judicial appointments disqualify from membership of the House of Commons. This is also true of the devolved institutions in the UK.

Judiciary and executive

The Lord Chancellor is head of the judiciary and is entitled to preside over the House of Lords which is the final court of appeal in the UK (again, subject to change by the Constitutional Reform Act 2005). But he is also a member of the UK Cabinet and a supporter of the political party in power.

Control

The executive to a large extent controls the legislature. This is mainly due to the strong governments returned by the "first-past-the-post" electoral system, the strong party whip system and the Prime Minister's powers of patronage.

Executive and judiciary

There is a strict separation here (apart from the Lord Chancellor) and the separation and independence of the judiciary are assured by various means:

   (a) Judges are paid a fixed, annual salary which is not dependent on an annual vote in the House of Commons, and is charged to the

Consolidated Fund. Parliament is asked to approve occasional increases, and cannot reduce the salaries.

(b) Judges hold office *ad vitam aut culpam*, ie for life and during good behaviour.

(c) Judges are protected from actions of defamation under the law of privilege, ensuring that they can speak freely in judgment.

Judiciary and legislature

The vast majority of judges are ineligible to be elected. In addition, English judges can only be removed from office by addresses from both Houses of Parliament, and indeed there has been only one example of this since 1700 (Jonah Barrington, an Irish judge, was removed in 1830). According to the doctrine of parliamentary sovereignty, the UK Parliament can, by passing legislation, nullify judicial decisions both prospectively and retrospectively. So, in that sense, the judiciary is subordinate to the legislature.

Exercise of functions

Executive and legislature

Ministers (ie the Executive) have legislative powers in that they may make delegated legislation, for example statutory instruments. An especial concern in this respect has been the controversially increasing use of "Henry VIII" clauses by Ministers (as to which, see Chapter 4).

Executive and judiciary

Essential judicial functions such as the conduct of civil and criminal trials are dealt with by the judiciary. But many disputes are dealt with by tribunals which are staffed by people who are not judges, and who are appointed by the executive. These tribunals are exercising judicial functions, though in a less formal way than the court. Some matters are also dealt with by means of a public inquiry in which a reporter, appointed by the executive, or a Minister makes a decision in line with departmental policy after hearing all the relevant arguments.

Judiciary and legislature

Each House of Parliament has the power to enforce its own privileges and to punish those who offend them, ie acting as judge of a Member's conduct. In declaring and interpreting the law, the judges are making law either in areas of common law, or in statutory interpretation. Judicial decisions are an important source of law in areas of police powers, civil liberties and administrative law.

Position of the Lord Chancellor

Prior to June 2003, the Lord Chancellor was a member of the executive and had a seat in the Cabinet. He was also a member of the legislature, being Speaker of the House of Lords and also having a seat in the Lords. Furthermore, he was also head of the judiciary in England and Wales, a member of the House of Lords Appellate Committee, and a member of the Judicial Committee of the Privy Council. The Lord Chancellor's Department was also responsible for recommending individuals for appointment as judges in England and Wales. As a member of the Cabinet, the Lord Chancellor could not be politically impartial nor could he be impartial in his role as a Government spokesman in the House of Lords. Thus, there were many criticisms of the position of the Lord Chancellor, not least being the lack of impartiality in dealing with appointments to the judiciary.

In June 2003, the Prime Minister announced an end to the role of the Lord Chancellor as a judge and as Speaker of the House of Lords. A Department of Constitutional Affairs was established which incorporates most of the responsibilities of the Lord Chancellor's Department. Lord Falconer was appointed as Secretary of State for Constitutional Affairs with a seat in the Cabinet and also became Speaker of the House of Lords. As part of the same package of reforms, the Government announced the establishment of an independent statutory Judicial Appointments Commission, and the creation of a new Supreme Court to replace the appellate jurisdiction of the House of Lords.

The Supreme Court of the United Kingdom

In recent years there have been mounting calls for the creation of a new independent Supreme Court, separating the highest appeal court from the House of Lords and removing the Law Lords from the legislature. On 12 June 2003 the Government announced its intention to do so and, in late 2004, the Constitutional Reform Act 2005 received Royal Assent.

The Government believes that the new Supreme Court will reflect and enhance the independence of the judiciary from both the legislature and the executive. The decision to create the Supreme Court does not imply any dissatisfaction with the previous performance of the House of Lords as the UK's highest court of appeal; indeed, its judges have conducted themselves with the utmost integrity and independence throughout the years. However, the Government believes that the time has come to establish a new court regulated by statute as a body separate from Parliament. This will allow the UK to adhere more rigidly to the doctrine of the separation of powers.

The Supreme Court will be a United Kingdom body, legally separate from the courts of England and Wales, which will take over the judicial function of the Law Lords in the House of Lords, and from the Judicial Committee of the Privy Council. The Supreme Court will be the final court of appeal in all matters under English law, Welsh law (to the extent that the Welsh Assembly make laws for Wales that differ from those in England) and Northern Irish law. It will also be a court of record for appeals from the Court of Session in Scotland (there is no right of appeal beyond the High Court of Justiciary for criminal cases except in so far as devolution issues arise).

The court will be located in a building separate from the Houses of Parliament and after a lengthy survey of suitable sites, including Somerset House, it has been decided that the location for the new court will be Middlesex Guildhall, in Parliament Square, Westminster, which is currently a Crown Court. The court is expected to hold its first hearing in 2008.

INDEPENDENCE OF THE JUDICIARY

It is a fundamental constitutional concept that the judiciary ought to be separate from the executive, ie the Government. This is one aspect of the separation of powers which is unequivocally accepted in the UK constitution, while all others are modified. The principles of the rule of law, and equality before the law, dictate that justice be administered impartially and universally, and this would be jeopardised if the courts were subject to the pressure of Government. Thus, the independence of the judiciary is strictly preserved under the British constitution and, to this end, s 3 of the Constitutional Reform Act 2005 guarantees the independence of the judiciary in any part of the UK. Under this provision, Ministers must uphold the continued independence of the judiciary and must not seek to influence particular judicial decisions through any special access to the judiciary.

Although appointed in both Scotland and England by the executive, the judiciary is, by a combination of legal rules and extra-legal factors, clearly independent of both the executive and the legislature. The independence of the judiciary is widely recognised and, for that reason, the Government will occasionally entrust to members of the judiciary the task of conducting inquiries into events of political significance, for example Lord Fraser's inquiry in 2004 into the costs of the Scottish Parliament building.

Appointment of judges

Judicial appointments are a matter reserved to the executive. Lords of Appeal in Ordinary are appointed by the Queen, on the advice of the Prime Minister. The Lord President of the Court of Session and the Lord Justice-Clerk are also appointed by the Queen on the advice of the Prime Minister from a nomination of the First Minister. Other judges of the Court of Session, sheriffs and sheriffs principal are appointed by the Queen on the recommendation of the First Minister (after consultation with the Lord President). Since 2002, the First Minister must also consult and take advice from the Judicial Appointments Board for Scotland which has the remit of advertising judicial posts, interviewing potential candidates and providing a list of suitable candidates.

Rules concerning the removal of judges

Under common law, judges hold office *ad vitam aut culpam* – for life and during good behaviour. This rule has arisen partly from custom, and also from the Claim of Right 1689. The Judicial Pensions and Retirement Act 1993 has introduced a new retirement age for Court of Session judges and sheriffs of 70, with the possibility of an extension to 75.

In England, the removal process has been statutory since at least 1701, and the current legislation can be found in the Supreme Court Act 1981. Normally, judges in the supreme courts are removable by the Queen on receipt of an address presented to her by both Houses of Parliament. But the provisions of the 1981 Act do not extend to Scotland. Thus, up until the enactment of the Scotland Act 1998, there was no statutory mechanism for the removal of a Court of Session judge. Now, s 95 of the 1998 Act lays down a procedure for the removal of a Court of Session judge. A judge may be removed from office by the Queen on the recommendation of the First Minister. The First Minister may make such a recommendation only if the Parliament, on a motion made by the First Minister, resolves that it should be made. The First Minister may seek such a resolution only if he has received a written report from a tribunal constituted under s 95, concluding that the judge is unfit for office by reason of inability, neglect of duty or misbehaviour. Furthermore, if the report relates to either the Lord President or the Lord Justice-Clerk, then the First Minister must consult the Prime Minister before making a recommendation.

In the case of sheriffs, a statutory procedure has existed for some years. It is set out in the Sheriff Courts (Scotland) Act 1971, and empowers the Scottish Ministers, on receiving a report from the Lord President and the Lord Justice-Clerk, to suspend or remove any sheriff from office, on clearly defined grounds of inability, neglect of duty or misbehaviour. If removal is contemplated, then the order is laid before both Houses of Parliament.

Judicial privilege

Judges enjoy an absolute privilege in relation to actions of damages in delict. There is no right of action against the higher judiciary in what they do or say in their judicial capacity. The Crown Proceedings Act 1947 allows injured parties the right to sue the Crown, and seek a remedy or damages on the basis of vicarious liability for the actions of Crown servants. But s 2 of the 1947 Act clearly states that the Crown is not vicariously liable for acts or omissions of a member of the judiciary. Thus, judges continue to enjoy immunity at common law in actions of delict.

Judges also enjoy protection under the criminal law. At common law, it is a crime to slander a judge or magistrate in reference to his or her official conduct or capacity. Threatening a judge is also a crime, as is bribing a judge or attempting to do so.

Impartiality of judges

Judges are expected to abstain from political activities, and matters of public controversy generally. In 1955, the Lord Chancellor, Lord Kilmuir, laid down rules which sought to prevent judges from making appearances in any medium without first consulting the Lord Chancellor. Lord Kilmuir felt that this would allow judges to isolate themselves from the media and any controversies. The influence of the Kilmuir rules have been somewhat eroded today, in that the passage of time has seen judges publish memoirs, write articles, appear on broadcasts and generally let their opinions be known. In 1987, this led to Lord Mackay removing the need to seek permission from the Lord Chancellor and since then judges have become increasingly vocal on controversial subjects.

The political neutrality of the judiciary is ensured by their exclusion from the House of Commons and the Scottish Parliament, by virtue of statute. Judicial salaries are also charged on the Consolidated Fund, meaning that there is no need to seek annual authority from Parliament, and no opportunity to debate the matter.

SOVEREIGNTY OF PARLIAMENT

This is also known as the legislative supremacy of Parliament and means that Acts of the UK Parliament are superior to any other source of law, and that Parliament has unlimited law-making power. This peculiar concept marks out the UK from most other legislatures in the world.

The legal basis for the principle of parliamentary sovereignty

The traditional view is that of Dicey which can be summarised in the following three tenets:

(1) no Act of the Queen in Parliament can be held invalid by a court of law;
(2) no Parliament can bind its successors as to the form or content of subsequent legislation; and
(3) there is no distinction in terms of procedure between ordinary statutes and those of constitutional importance.

The importance of Dicey's tenets has been reflected in a number of important decisions. In *Pickin v British Railways Board* (1974), Pickin sought to challenge the validity of an Act of Parliament on the ground that Parliament had been misled during the course of the Bill through the legislature. The House of Lords held that no court of law can go behind an Act of Parliament, public or private, to investigate how it was introduced or what took place during its passage, even where irregularity or fraud was alleged.

In *Ellen Street Estates Ltd v Minister of Health* (1934), it was held that Parliament could not bind itself as to the form of subsequent legislation and could not properly enact that provisions in one statute could not be altered by a subsequent Act other than by express words. Maugham LJ stated:

> "The Legislature cannot, according to our constitution, bind itself as to the form of subsequent legislation, and it is impossible for Parliament to enact that in a subsequent statute dealing with the same subject-matter there can be no implied repeal. If in a subsequent Act, Parliament chooses to make it plain that the earlier statute is being to some extent repealed, effect must be given to that intention just because it is the will of the Legislature."

However, some matters authorised by legislation are of such a nature that they cannot be undone by a subsequent Act of Parliament. For example, s 4 of the Statute of Westminster 1931 states that no Act of Parliament passed after 1931 shall extend to a Dominion unless it is declared in the Act that the Dominion has requested and consented to it. This appears to acknowledge a territorial limit to the sovereignty of Parliament.

Practical limitations on parliamentary sovereignty

The possibility of disobedience

Though Parliament successfully enacted the poll tax legislation (the Abolition of Domestic Rates etc (Scotland) Act 1987 for Scotland and the Local Government Finance Act 1988 for England and Wales) the widespread disobedience and non-payment forced Parliament to repeal the legislation and introduce a more acceptable alternative. Dicey calls the possibility of disobedience an "external limitation on the sovereignty of Parliament".

The beliefs and opinions of MPs

The Government is unlikely to propose a piece of legislation which will not receive the support of Members of Parliament. Legislation cannot progress through the Parliament unless it has the support of a majority of MPs.

Consultation with interested parties

In consulting interest groups, the Government may bring about more acceptable legislation. For example, the British Veterinary Association was consulted in relation to the Dangerous Dogs Act 1991. Thus, consultation may inform and alter the content of appropriate legislation.

International agreements and world status

Since 1966, the UK has recognised the rights of the individual under the European Convention on Human Rights. The Convention has also been incorporated into the domestic law of the United Kingdom by virtue of the Human Rights Act 1998. Under the 1998 Act, the House of Lords, the Judicial Committee of the Privy Council, the English High Court, the Court of Appeal, the Court of Session and the High Court of Justiciary (operating in an appeal capacity) have the ability to make declarations that an Act of the UK Parliament is incompatible with the provisions of the Convention. However, these declarations, though likely to be politically embarrassing, are non-binding.

Limitations arising from membership of the EU

As a result of its membership of the European Union, the UK has agreed to be bound by European law. The European Communities Act 1972 ensures the applicability of European law in the UK and states that all directly effective EU legislation creates an enforceable right within the UK and must be enforced by all courts and tribunals. It also states that all UK law must be applied subject to European law. Therefore, European law overarches our system of national law and, if there is any conflict, it is European law which prevails.

These provisions are fairly revolutionary in that they fundamentally undermine the concept of parliamentary sovereignty and the supremacy of the UK Parliament. The implications of the European Communities Act 1972 were discussed in great detail in the case of *R v Secretary of State for Transport, ex p Factortame (No 2)* (1991). On appeal, it was affirmed by the House of Lords that an Act of Parliament contradicting EU legislation could not be enforced in the courts of the UK. Furthermore, since EU law had to be enforced, courts were entitled to issue orders to such effect. In effect, the 1972 Act allows European legislation to take precedence over that of the UK. There have been many positive effects of this principle, and some areas of UK law have been fundamentally changed for the better because of the influence of European law.

THE RULE OF LAW

The rule of law is a nebulous concept. It is not a legal doctrine as such but is more philosophical in form. The rule of law means that matters should be regulated by law, not by force, and in this form the principle is common to all civilised societies. In *X v Morgan Grampian Ltd* (1991), Lord Bridge said: "The maintenance of the rule of law is in every way as important in a free society as the democratic franchise. In our society the rule of law rests upon twin foundations: the sovereignty of the Queen in Parliament in making the law and the sovereignty of the Queen's courts in interpreting and applying the law."

In modern times the concept has become encapsulated in the following principles:

(1) An absence of arbitrary power: officials must be able to show legal authority for their actions whether they be police constables or Ministers of the Crown.

(2) Legal rights and duties must be determined, protected and enforced by the ordinary courts in accordance with the ordinary law. Where rights are determined by bodies other than courts, such as tribunals, the proceedings of the decision-making body should be characterised by openness, fairness and impartiality.

(3) The rights of individuals must yield to the rights of society as a whole only in accordance with specific rules of law recognised by the ordinary courts. The emphasis is on the rights of the individual.

(4) There must be clearly defined limits within which discretionary power is exercised. There has been an increasing practice of conferring discretionary powers on Ministers by giving them authority to make delegated legislation. It is important that limits are set and adhered to.

(5) There must be adequate safeguards for human rights.

MINISTERIAL RESPONSIBILITY

The doctrine of ministerial responsibility performs the function of securing a level of accountability and control over the executive by Parliament. There are two aspects of responsibility: collective and individual. Under the doctrine of collective ministerial responsibility, all Ministers must accept Cabinet decisions, or dissent publicly and resign, unless collective responsibility is waived by the Cabinet on a particular issue. This mechanism allows Governments to show a united front to Parliament and the public. Collective responsibility is followed slavishly by Governments since the executive must be seen as strong and there can be no doubt over its policies. Thus, if a Minister is placed under parliamentary pressure on a particular issue, the remainder of the Government will rally to give support, since the policy will be a common one.

On the other hand, individual ministerial responsibility ensures that Ministers are responsible to Parliament for the administration of their individual departments, ie a Minister is accountable for not only personal decisions but also the actions and decisions of civil servants. The most infamous example of this doctrine can be found in the Crichel Down Affair where the Air Ministry had compulsorily purchased land for defence purposes in 1938. By 1954, the land was no longer required and it was transferred to the Ministry of Agriculture which ultimately let it out to a tenant. The original owner of the land was neither consulted nor offered the opportunity to regain ownership. An inquiry into the affair discovered that many other land owners had been similarly affected and that the Ministry had acted in an underhand fashion. This resulted in widespread parliamentary and public condemnation and the Minister for Agriculture, Thomas Dugdale, resigned, taking full responsibility for the actions of his department. Similarly, in 1982, the Foreign Secretary, Lord Carrington, took personal responsibility for mismanagement of the Foreign and Commonwealth Office in failing to appreciate the threat of Argentine invasion of the Falklands.

In most cases, attempts are made to invoke ministerial responsibility by parliamentary questions or debate. In this way, parliamentary criticism can lead to public condemnation and might cause a resignation, but such resignations are becoming increasingly rare. In modern times, there has been a blurring of the distinction between questions of mismanagement and personal behaviour, and many resignations since 1945 have in fact involved questions of personal conduct, such as those of John Profumo in 1963 (who lied to the House), and David Mellor in 1992 who was eventually forced out of the Cabinet following a war of attrition with the newspapers over his moral conduct. More recently, the former Home Secretary, David Blunkett, was forced to resign after his private life led to the alleged speeding up of an immigration application for the nanny of his son.

In recent years, given the growth in the number of executive Next Steps Agencies, the notion of ministerial responsibility has been identified with the idea of ministerial accountability, and a policy/operational dichotomy has developed in some government departments. Thus, the blame for many acts of mismanagement within a government department may be attached to the agency head or civil servant directorate involved instead of, or as well as, the Minister. Corrective action within the department will, however, be undertaken by the Minister.

ESSENTIAL FACTS

- The doctrine of the separation of powers recognises three separate organs of government, namely the legislature, the executive and the judiciary. Each organ should be vested with one main function of government only and should not interfere with the functions of another.
- It is debatable to what extent the separation of powers truly exists in the UK since there are a number of areas of overlap. In particular, the office of Lord Chancellor has been a constant refutation of the doctrine, however, this has been altered by the Constitutional Reform Act 2005.
- The independence of the judiciary is a fundamental principle of the UK constitution. Judges must be free from the pressure of government in order to achieve fairness and impartiality and to this end their security of tenure is protected by a number of legal rules and Acts of Parliament.
- Parliamentary sovereignty or the legislative supremacy of Parliament means that Acts of the UK Parliament are superior to any other source of law and that Parliament has unlimited law-making power.

- In modern times, parliamentary sovereignty has been somewhat eroded by a number of practical limitations, such as the UK's membership of the EU, and other international obligations.
- The rule of law is common to all civilised societies and represents an absence of arbitrary power. The rule of law recognises all citizens as being equal before the law and ensures that all state action is authorised by law.
- Countries which subscribe to the rule of law ought to have adequate safeguards in place to protect citizens from abuse of discretionary power and should also be able to protect fundamental human rights.
- Ministerial responsibility ensures that Ministers are responsible to Parliament for the administration of their individual departments, ie a Minister is accountable for not only personal decisions but also the actions and decisions of civil servants.
- In most cases, attempts are made to invoke ministerial responsibility by parliamentary questions or debate. In this way, parliamentary criticism can lead to public condemnation and may cause a resignation, but such resignations are becoming increasingly rare.

ESSENTIAL CASES

Pickin v British Railways Board (1974): no court has the power to disregard an Act of Parliament or question parliamentary procedure.

Ellen Street Estates Ltd v Minister of Health (1934): Parliament cannot bind itself as to the form of subsequent legislation or properly enact that provisions in one statute cannot be altered by a subsequent Act other than by express words.

R v Secretary of State for Transport, ex p Factortame (No 2) (1991): in effect confirms the practical limitations placed upon parliamentary sovereignty by EU membership. The European Communities Act 1972 Act allows European legislation to take precedence over that of the UK.

X v Morgan Grampian Ltd (1991): description of the rule of law.

3 STRUCTURE OF GOVERNMENT IN THE UK

In order to understand the context within which administrative law operates, it is necessary to gain an understanding of the structure of government within the United Kingdom. It is important to be able to identify the sources of power within the framework of the UK constitution since administrative law is essentially directed by the actions of government and the ways in which public authorities exercise powers which have been delegated to them. The purpose of this chapter is to give the reader an overview of the principal institutions of government within the UK and to outline the source and extent of their powers.

CENTRAL GOVERNMENT

Government in the UK spends on average 40 per cent of national income per year. The money is spent by government departments on administration and services provided by independent or executive agencies or other bodies, as well as on the regulatory functions supervised by government departments. The term "government" is generally taken to denote the executive organs of the state, the civil services, and the armed forces. Strictly speaking, it is not in itself a legal entity and is rarely referred to in legislation or case law. Instead, the term "the Crown" is used when referring to central government acting in its executive capacity, and all actions, whether they be derived from primary or secondary legislation, or the Royal Prerogative, are carried on in the name of the Crown. The Crown in turn denotes the Sovereign who has a key role in the summoning, proroguing and dissolving of Parliament. The Queen is in fact part of Parliament and, strictly speaking, Acts of Parliament are Acts of the Queen in Parliament. All Bills passing through Parliament must receive the Royal Assent of the Sovereign before they can become a formal Act of Parliament.

Central government departments

Government departments have the responsibility of carrying out the core functions of government in the UK. They initiate the vast majority of Government legislation and have powers and functions laid out by statute, subject to some ministerial powers which are exercised by virtue of the Royal Prerogative. Departments have a clear structure and are headed by a Minister or Secretary of State who is assisted by civil servants in the formulation of policy and legislation. The doctrine of ministerial responsibility ensures that Ministers are ultimately accountable to Parliament for the actions of their departments and officials.

The Ministers of the Crown Act 1975 allows for departments to be restructured and responsibilities to be transferred through Order in Council. These powers have been utilised on a number of occasions in order to reflect ever-changing policy objectives within government. The degree of discretion available to government departments can be considerable and, besides ministerial responsibility, they are also subject to scrutiny by the Parliamentary Commissioner for Administration concerning instances of maladministration.

Non-departmental public bodies

Non-departmental public bodies (NDPBs) can be found in various forms and include the National Health Service, public corporations such as the BBC, and Next Steps Agencies. An important development in the organisation of governmental functions can be seen in the creation of Next Steps Agencies. They have responsibility for the execution of policy on a day-to-day basis and high levels of responsibility are delegated to agency managers. Their powers are set down in framework agreements made between the relevant department and the agency concerned. The agreement will outline present and future objectives for the agency, financial arrangements, personnel and staffing policy and review procedures. The head of a Next Steps Agency is the Chief Executive, who is appointed on a contract of employment limited to around 5 years in duration.

The exact position of Next Steps Agencies is uncertain and one of the criticisms of their growing use is the perceived lack of accountability to Parliament. The Government, however, is assured that accountability is achieved through Agency Chief Executives being accountable to the relevant Minister who, in turn, is accountable to Parliament. Their work is also scrutinised by Select Committees and the Public Accounts Committee.

In addition, there are a number of other quasi-autonomous governmental bodies known as "quangos". Such bodies are invariably created by statute and well-known examples include the Scottish Development Agency, the Equal Opportunities Commission and the Civil Aviation Authority. As creatures of statute, quangos must keep within their statutory powers, and may be controlled by the courts if they act outwith those statutory powers. Ministers may also issue directions or guidelines regulating the behaviour of such bodies. Quangos are often criticised as being unelected and unaccountable since they are outwith the scope of mainstream political control and their members are appointed by the Government.

Accountability

It should be noted that although there may be issues surrounding the accountability of non-departmental public bodies, their status and powers ultimately emanate from statute, meaning that they are all subject to control by the courts. Thus the decisions of all such bodies may be challenged on the ground of acting *ultra vires*.

DEVOLVED GOVERNMENT

One of the key policies of the present Labour Government has been the devolution of central government power to the nations and regions of the UK. The Report of the Royal Commission on the Constitution (the Kilbrandon Commission) defined "devolution" as "the delegation of central government powers without the relinquishment of sovereignty". Thus, devolution means that powers are conferred on a devolved institution by the central legislature, but that legislature retains residual power to legislate in respect of the devolved areas, even though that power will in all probability not be used. In the UK, devolution has been given to Scotland, Wales and Northern Ireland, each to varying degrees.

As far as Scotland is concerned, devolution has been given by virtue of the Scotland Act 1998 which establishes a Scottish Parliament with devolved law-making powers. In strict legal terms, however, the UK Parliament has the power to abolish the Scottish Parliament by repeal of the Scotland Act. It may also add powers to, or remove powers from, the Scottish Parliament through a piece of subsequent legislation amending the Scotland Act. Thus, a devolved legislature, like the Scottish Parliament, is subordinate to the central legislature. This differs markedly from federalism, where the central legislature is said to be co-ordinate (or have equal status) with the regional legislatures. A characteristic of the federal system of government is that both the central legislature and the regional bodies will be regulated by a written constitution, unlike the position in the UK. Furthermore, under a federal system of government, the regional institutions have the same powers under the constitution. This is markedly in contrast with the UK where the Scottish Parliament has the power to vary taxes by up to three pence in the pound yet the National Assembly for Wales has no equivalent powers under the Government of

Wales Act 1998. The Scottish Parliament also has the power to pass Acts (even if these are properly classified as subordinate legislation), whereas the National Assembly for Wales may pass only statutory instruments; both, however, are challengeable in the courts as being *ultra vires* (for a discussion of Acts of the Scottish Parliament and the *ultra vires* doctrine, see Chapter 4).

Composition of the Scottish Parliament

The Scottish Parliament is a unicameral (one chamber only) legislature, with 129 members. The Parliament sits for a fixed term of 4 years, though there are provisions to allow for extraordinary Scottish general elections before the expiry of this term, if the Parliament cannot nominate a First Minister within 28 days, or if at least two-thirds of all MSPs vote for an early dissolution of the Parliament.

Powers and functions

Under s 28 of the Scotland Act 1998, the Scottish Parliament has the power to make laws, known as Acts of the Scottish Parliament (asps). These may be in relation to any of the devolved matters, such as health, education, housing, local government or the environment, and may amend previous Acts of the UK Parliament which deal with devolved matters in Scotland. The Parliament cannot legislate in respect of matters reserved to the UK Parliament and the list of reserved matters is contained in Sch 5 to the Act. It includes areas such as the constitution, foreign affairs, social security and defence.

The Scotland Act does not list devolved matters; rather, it lists reserved matters. This means that everything that is not reserved is devolved by implication. This is known as the *retaining model* of devolution and should result in fewer disputes between the Scottish Parliament, central government and the courts as to the competence of the Parliament to pass particular Acts.

The Scottish Parliament also has the power to increase or decrease the basic rate of income tax by three pence in the pound and to determine spending priorities within the Scottish block or assigned budget.

The Scottish Executive

An important responsibility of the Scottish Parliament is the nomination of the First Minster and the approval of other Ministers. Under s 45 of the Scotland Act 1998, the First Minister is appointed by the Monarch on the proposal of the Presiding Officer (Speaker of the Parliament), who forwards the name of the person nominated by the Scottish Parliament, following a vote if necessary. Ministers and Junior Ministers are appointed by the First Minister, with the approval of the Monarch and, more importantly, after obtaining the approval of the Scottish Parliament. The Scottish Executive has assumed the functions and responsibilities of the previous Scottish Office Ministers in so far as they relate to devolved matters, though the allocation of these responsibilities and functions is a matter for the First Minister and the Parliament.

LOCAL GOVERNMENT

Local government is a creature of statute and so may be created, restructured or abolished by an Act of Parliament. In Scotland, local government is a devolved area and may be altered by means of an Act of the Scottish Parliament. The Scottish Parliament may not, however, abolish the franchise in its entirety. In Scotland, the single-tier system of 32 local councils established by the Local Government etc (Scotland) Act 1994 took effect on 1 April 1996. Scottish councils have responsibility for education, social work, planning, housing, roads and transport, licensing and many other functions. They also have statutory powers to pass byelaws, management rules and other orders for defined purposes, and limited powers to raise local taxes, mainly through the council tax.

Local government only possesses those powers and functions which are conferred to it by statute, and any activity taken outwith those powers is *ultra vires* or unlawful. By virtue of the Local Government in Scotland Act 2003, Scottish local authorities now have an additional power to do anything which is likely to promote or advance the well-being of their area and any persons within that area. This includes the power to incur extra expenditure, enter into contractual agreements, facilitate activities and give financial assistance. The power to advance well-being is, however, subject to limits and guidance provided by the Scottish Ministers. For example, the power may not be used to duplicate services, raise taxation or override existing statutory provisions which limit local authority powers. If a local authority exceeds its powers, the Scottish Ministers may issue an enforcement direction requiring the authority to remedy the abuse of power.

ESSENTIAL FACTS

- The structure of government in the UK consists of several tiers: central government, devolved government and local government.

- The term "government" is generally taken to denote the executive organs of the state, the civil services and the armed forces. It is not in itself a legal entity and is rarely referred to in legislation or case law. Instead, the term "the Crown" is used when referring to central government acting in its executive capacity.

- Government departments have the responsibility of carrying out the core functions of government in the UK. They initiate the vast majority of Government legislation and have powers and functions laid out by statute, subject to some ministerial powers which are exercised by virtue of the Royal Prerogative.

- Non-departmental public bodies (NDPBs) can be found in various forms and include the National Health Service, public corporations such as the BBC, and Next Steps Agencies. They have responsibility for the execution of policy on a day-to-day basis.

- The decisions of NDPBs may be challenged in court as *ultra vires* with regard to their enabling legislation.

- Devolution has been afforded to Scotland by virtue of the Scotland Act 1998 which creates the Scottish Parliament, the Executive and the Administration. The Scottish Parliament is subordinate to the United Kingdom Parliament.

- Section 28 of the Scotland Act 1998 allows the Scottish Parliament to make laws known as Acts of the Scottish Parliament (asps). Such Acts may properly be categorised as subordinate legislation and may be challenged in court as being outwith the competence of the Scottish Parliament, or *ultra vires*. They may also be challenged utilising the procedure for devolution issues in Sch 6 to the Scotland Act 1998.

- Local government is a creature of statute and may be created, restructured or abolished by an Act of Parliament. In Scotland, local government is a devolved area and may be altered by means of an Act of the Scottish Parliament.

- Local government only possesses those powers and functions which are conferred to it by statute, and any activity taken outwith those powers is *ultra vires* or unlawful. The Local Government in Scotland Act 2003 gives local authorities an additional power to do anything which is likely to promote or advance the well-being of their area and any persons within that area, subject to limits and guidance provided by the Scottish Ministers.

4 SUBORDINATE LEGISLATION

It is common for Acts of Parliament to confer on Ministers or other executive bodies the power to make rules and regulations which have the force of law and are thus properly called legislation. The phrase "subordinate legislation" covers every exercise of such power which is sometimes also known as "delegated" or "secondary" legislation. The power to enact such legislation comes from an authorising or "parent" Act which will be an Act of Parliament. There are many types of subordinate legislation; however, the most common are statutory instruments, Orders in Council, byelaws of local authorities and other bodies, regulations, rules and codes of practice. Acts of the Scottish Parliament, Acts of the Northern Ireland Assembly and legislation of the National Assembly for Wales are also forms of subordinate legislation, since a parent Act confers the law-making powers in all three cases, ie s 28 of the Scotland Act 1998, s 5 of the Northern Ireland Act 1998 and s 22 of the Government of Wales Act 1998.

TRADITIONAL JUSTIFICATIONS

There are a number of traditional advantages proffered for the use of subordinate legislation in the UK. They can be usefully summarised as follows:

- Parliament only has time to concern itself with the broad principles of Acts. Detailed regulations and rules should be dealt with by the administration. The Road Traffic Acts are a good example: the Road Traffic Act 1972 empowered the Secretary of State to make regulations for the use of vehicles on public roads. Such detail cannot possibly be set out in an Act of Parliament. Thus subordinate legislation can save parliamentary time and lead to legislative efficiency.
- Subordinate legislation allows the knowledge and experience available outside Parliament to be utilised through appropriate consultation. For example, in issuing regulations under the Dangerous Dogs Act 1991, the Secretary of State must consult with the British Veterinary Association.
- In times of emergency, it is impossible to pass an Act of Parliament quickly enough to deal with the situation. Subordinate legislation can be passed rapidly and allows responsiveness to emergencies. For

example, the Secretary of State for the Environment could restrict the movement of livestock if there was an outbreak of Foot and Mouth Disease.

- Subordinate legislation is also used to give effect to Acts of Parliament. Often an Act of Parliament will state that all, or some, of the Act is to come into force on a date to be set by the Secretary of State. This is done using a statutory instrument which is known as a "commencement order".

GENERAL PRINCIPLES OF LEGALITY

There are a number of general principles of law which apply to every use of subordinate legislation within the UK. First, it is accepted that matters of principle must be dealt with through Acts of Parliament and not by means of subordinate legislation. An example of this can be found in the Health and Safety at Work etc Act 1974. The Act itself deals with the fundamental legal principles, ie that there should be a Health and Safety Executive with powers of regulation and supervision over workplace safety. However, the detail and minutiae of rules of safety for each place of work are issued through subordinate legislation in the from of regulations, eg the Diving at Work Regulations 1997.

It is a further constitutional principle that taxation may not be imposed via subordinate legislation. Parliamentary approval is always necessary for the imposition of taxation. In *Attorney-General v Wilts United Dairies* (1922), a charge of an extra 2d per gallon of milk was introduced by the Food Controller who was empowered to issue regulations for the production and distribution of milk. The increased charge only applied to one particular trading zone and the House of Lords regarded this as a tax for which no clear statutory authority existed.

Only Parliament should have the power to override or alter a provision of an Act of Parliament. To do so by subordinate legislation is regarded as constitutionally unsound. Nevertheless, such power has occasionally been conferred on Ministers. For example, s 30 of the Scotland Act 1998 allows for Schs 4 and 5 to the Act to be modified by Order in Council. This allows changes to be made to the content of these Schedules without the necessity of passing another Act of Parliament. Such exercise of power is known as a "Henry VIII clause"; so named since King Henry is popularly regarded as the epitome of executive autocracy.

Since the recommendations of the Donoughmore Committee (1932), Henry VIII clauses have only been used where necessary and not purely for convenience. However, a recent controversial development has seen moves to make amendments to primary legislation by subordinate means commonplace. The Legislative and Regulatory Reform Bill proposes to give Ministers power to alter *any* law passed by Parliament. The only limitations are that new crimes cannot be created if the penalty is greater than 2 years in prison, and that taxation cannot be increased. But any other law will be subject to change, no matter how important. The Government claims that the new powers will only be used for uncontroversial issues, but no such safeguard exists in the Bill, leading commentators satirically to re-name it the "Abolition of Parliament Bill".

When Parliament has given subordinate power to a person or body then power should be exercised only by the person authorised. Sub-delegation to another body is improper and is reflected in the Latin maxim *delegatus non potest delegare* – a delegate cannot delegate further. This is because it is assumed that the person or body designated to exercise a power has been chosen for their qualities and suitability for the task in question. In *Vine v National Dock Labour Board* (1957), the Labour Board had powers relating to discipline derived from statute which were sub-delegated to a disciplinary committee composed of some of its members. Using these powers, the Board proceeded to sack Vine who challenged the validity of the decision. The House of Lords held that disciplinary powers could not be sub-delegated but did recognise that the rule against sub-delegation was not absolute. In fact, delegation is possible in certain circumstances, for example where powers of a Minister are validly executed by individuals within a department. Unless the "parent" Act specifically excludes such delegation then this will be valid.

Subordinate legislation must not be retrospective in operation. In *Malloch v Aberdeen Corporation* (1974), the Secretary of State, under his power to make regulations prescribing the standards to which local education authorities conformed, attempted to alter the status of certified teachers who were already in employment. The Court of Session held that such use of delegated power was invalid.

Finally, the right to seek redress before the courts must not be denied by subordinate legislation unless expressly authorised by the parent Act. In *Chester v Bateson* (1920), there existed a wide statutory power to issue regulations for securing public safety and the defence of the realm during World War I. A regulation was issued to prevent munitions workers being evicted from their homes. To take court proceedings for the recovery of such a house without the Minister's consent was made an offence. The High Court held that this was *ultra vires* (outwith his powers), and that access to the courts could not be taken away except with the express authority of Parliament.

STATUTORY INSTRUMENTS

The most common forms of subordinate legislation are statutory instruments (which can also take the form of Regulations, Rules and Orders) and the power to make them will be delegated to a Minister by an Act of Parliament. There also exists a variation on the statutory instrument, known as an Order in Council. Orders in Council refer to the Privy Council which advises the Queen on matters of constitutional importance. There are two types of Order in Council: those made under the authority of the Royal Prerogative, and those which are delegated to Ministers through an Act of Parliament. The first is an Order which is made without requiring the consent of Parliament and is usually reserved for matters of constitutional importance such as the dissolution of Parliament. They are made by the Privy Council with the authority of the Queen; although the Queen's assent today is purely formal and in reality is decided by Ministers. The second type of Order is authorised by an Act of Parliament and cannot be made without parliamentary approval. Such an Order was used to transfer powers from the UK Ministers to the Scottish Parliament under the devolution settlement. Orders in Council do not practically differ in status from that of statutory instruments. However, through custom, Orders in Council are regarded as being more dignified and are therefore used for matters of constitutional importance.

Controls

Around 3,500 statutory instruments are passed every year. Some of these are very short and simple, such as a commencement order bringing into force the provisions of an Act of Parliament, whereas others are long and complex. This gives rise to the question of how these vast powers conferred on Ministers are to be reconciled with the process of democratic scrutiny and control. There are, however, several recognised means of control.

Consultation of interests

Consultation may be voluntary, but frequently there is a statutory obligation to consult relevant persons or bodies as laid down in the parent Act. Sometimes the Act will specify the bodies that must be consulted. For example, s 2(4) of the Dangerous Dogs Act 1991 states that the Secretary of State must consult with such persons or bodies as appear to have relevant knowledge or experience, including a body concerned with animal welfare, a body concerned with veterinary science and practice, and a body concerned with breeds of dogs. Practically speaking, this translates into the need to consult the RSPCA, the British Veterinary Association and the Kennel Club.

In practice, Government Ministers and departments consult widely. The special knowledge or experience of those consulted is intended to make subordinate legislation both more workable and acceptable to those who are affected by it.

Parliamentary controls

The Act of Parliament which grants the power to make delegated legislation will often specify a parliamentary procedure to be followed. The parent Act may simply require a statutory instrument made under it to be "laid before Parliament" with no other procedural requirement. "Laying" simply means that a copy of the statutory instrument must be delivered to the Votes and Proceedings Office in the Houses of Parliament. Normally the statutory instrument is laid before both Houses, but in some cases (for example where taxation is involved) it might be laid before the Commons only.

Alternatively, the parent Act may state that a statutory instrument is to be subject to annulment in performance of a resolution of either House (or the Commons only). Such an instrument may be annulled within a period of 40 days starting from the day when it is laid. If it is not annulled within that period, the instrument comes into force on the date specified. This is known as the *negative procedure* and is a fairly weak form of control.

Conversely, a statutory instrument may be subject to the affirmative approval of Parliament before coming into effect. Here, a motion approving the instrument must be passed by both Houses (or the Commons only) within a specified period, usually either 28 or 40 days. This is known as the *affirmative procedure* and is obviously a stronger form of control.

Some statutory instruments have no procedural requirements at all. This is not uncommon and an example can be found in commencement orders which are invariably not required to be laid before Parliament since they are merely bringing into force provisions of an Act of Parliament.

Examination by Parliamentary Committees

Since 1973 there has been a Joint Committee on Statutory Instruments (also known as the Joint Scrutiny Committee) consisting of seven members of each House of Parliament. Its role is to consider all instruments laid before each House (Commons members only deal with Commons-only instruments). The Committee then decides whether the attention of each House (or Commons only where appropriate) should be drawn to any instrument on one or more of the following grounds:

(a) that it imposes a charge on public revenues;

(b) that it seeks to oust the right of challenge in the courts;

(c) that it purports to have retrospective effect;

(d) that there has been an unjustifiable delay in laying or publication;

(e) where it is suspected to be *ultra vires*;

(f) that its form or purpose requires explanation;

(g) that its drafting appears to be defective; or

(h) on any other ground that does not impinge on the merits or policy behind it.

There are also Standing Committees on statutory instruments appointed to consider the merits of such instruments or drafts as may be referred to them by the House. Such committees can debate the instrument for a maximum of 90 minutes but the merits cannot themselves be voted upon. The Government may then take account of the views expressed, although it is under no obligation to do so, and no debate may take place on the floor of the House. These procedures have received widespread criticism from many MPs and they provide very little in the way of real control.

Publicity

Publicity is a form of control in that it allows the public to have access to the legislation and so any irregularities may easily come to light. It is a statutory requirement by virtue of s 2(1) of the Statutory Instruments Act 1946 that all instruments be published. As soon as an instrument is made it is sent to The Stationery Office, where it is numbered, printed and made available for public sale. There are a small number of circumstances where an instrument may be exempt from publication, such as where it would be unnecessary because the brevity of the period for which it is to be in force, or where it would be contrary to public interest to have it published (for which ministerial authorisation is required).

Challenge in the courts

Challenge in the courts is not possible for Acts of Parliament, but it is for delegated legislation. This is because the legislative powers of the UK Parliament are unlimited (at least in terms of UK law) whereas those of Ministers are not. There are two main grounds of challenge both of which are discussed in detail in Chapter 4:

(a) that the content or substance of the instrument is *ultra vires* the parent Act, ie goes beyond the powers authorised by the Act; or

(b) that the correct procedures have not been followed in the making of the instrument.

ACTS OF THE SCOTTISH PARLIAMENT

Acts of the Scottish Parliament (asps) are a form of delegated legislation, since the power to make an asp comes from Act of Parliament, namely s 28 of the Scotland Act 1998. They are open to challenge in the courts if they infringe any of the provisions of s 29 of the 1998 Act, ie that they are outwith the competence of the Scottish Parliament and so *ultra vires*. Section 29(2) outlines the circumstances in which a measure would be outwith the competence of the Scottish Parliament – if:

(a) it would form part of the law of a country or territory other than Scotland;

(b) its effect would be to modify any provision of the Scotland Act (or other statutes of constitutional note listed in Sch 4);

(c) it relates to reserved matters (laid out in great detail in Sch 5, eg defence, foreign affairs, succession to the throne etc);

(d) it is incompatible with any of the rights under the European Convention on Human Rights or with EC law; or

(e) it would remove the Lord Advocate from his position as head of the system of prosecution and investigation of deaths in Scotland.

In terms of Sch 5 to the Scotland Act 1998, there are a number of areas which are known as "reserved" areas and here the Scottish Parliament has no power. The reserved areas are split into both "general" and "specific" reservations. General reservations deal with subjects such as defence, social security and foreign affairs. They are areas where the law generally needs to be the same across the UK or must be retained in order to fulfil international obligations. Specific reservations are very detailed and provide particular areas where the Scottish Parliament has no power. The list is long and includes such areas as abortion; space exploration; alteration of time zones; and xeno-transplantation.

In order to ensure that the Scottish Parliament legislates within its proper spheres of competence, there are numerous provisions in the Scotland Act to allow pre-Assent scrutiny of Bills. Ministers presenting Bills to the Scottish Parliament must make a declaration that, in their opinion, the Bill is within the legislative competence of the Scottish Parliament. There are similar provisions contained in the Human Rights Act 1998 for the making of declarations of compatibility with the ECHR by Scottish Ministers. The Presiding Officer has also been given the power to prevent a Bill being introduced to the Scottish Parliament if in his or her view it would be outwith the competence of the Parliament. This power could, however, be overruled by the Scottish Parliament.

The question of whether a Bill, or any provision, is within the legislative competence of the Parliament may also be referred to the Judicial Committee of the Privy Council by one of the following Law Officers: the Lord Advocate, the Attorney-General or the Advocate-General. This must take place within 4 weeks of the Bill completing its stages in the Scottish Parliament.

Furthermore, the Secretary of State for Scotland may prohibit a Bill from being submitted for Royal Assent if he or she has reasonable grounds to believe that it would be incompatible with any international obligations, or if the Bill would have an adverse effect on the operation of an enactment as it applies to reserved matters. In this case, the Secretary of State must identify the specific provisions concerned, and must give reasons for his or her decision. This power is similarly invested in any Secretary of State of the UK Government.

Devolution issues

Despite the safeguards in place to ensure that the Scottish Parliament legislates within its powers, there is always the possibility that provisions may slip through the net which are potentially outwith the competence of the Parliament. Accordingly, Sch 6 to the Scotland Act 1998 sets out provisions as to how a "devolution issue" should be handled. Part I of Sch 6 defines a devolution issue as "a question whether an Act of the Scottish Parliament or any provision of an Act of the Scottish Parliament is within the legislative competence of the Parliament". Such an issue can arise before any court or tribunal, in civil or in criminal cases.

In *A (A Mental Patient) v Scottish Ministers* (2000), a devolution issue was raised in an appeal by A, who had been held in Carstairs without limit of time under a mental health detention order. A had appealed against the refusal of the Scottish Ministers to discharge him from Carstairs. Under the Mental Health (Scotland) Act 1984, detention was allowed only where the detainee's behaviour resulted from a mental condition which was likely to be alleviated by treatment. Subsequent to A's original detention, the Mental Health (Public Safety and Appeals) (Scotland) Act 1999 amended the 1984 Act so that discharge could be refused where the Scottish Ministers were satisfied that continued detention, whether for treatment or not, was justified to protect the public from serious harm.

The question raised was whether it was incompetent for the Scottish Parliament to pass the 1999 Act because the potential incompatibility with the right to liberty under Art 5 of the European Convention on Human Rights 1950. As the 1999 Act was passed after A had lodged his appeal, the court also considered whether the 1999 Act could be relied on retrospectively to authorise A's continued detention on the ground that it was necessary in order to protect the public from serious harm, where under previous legislation A would have been entitled to a discharge.

The Court held, answering the devolution issues in the negative, that the right to liberty was not absolute and had to be balanced against the duty imposed on Governments under Art 2 of the Convention to protect life and health. As long as the court was satisfied under the 1984 Act that there was a risk of serious harm to the public, continued detention was justified and did not contravene A's human rights and retrospective application of the 1999 Act amendment was legitimate.

Subordinate legislation of the Scottish Parliament

The Scotland Act 1998 conveys powers to make subordinate legislation upon Scottish Ministers, Ministers of the Crown, and Her Majesty in Council. This is necessary for the same reasons that the UK Parliament requires power to enact statutory instruments and Orders in Council. Statutory instruments of the Scottish Parliament are known as Scottish statutory instruments or SSIs. Although Scottish Ministers normally make subordinate legislation only in areas where the Parliament has legislative competence, provisions exist which also allow them to legislate in areas where the Parliament has no competence. The Scotland Act allows a UK Minister to transfer functions, by Order in Council, to Scottish Ministers and these functions may then be exercised in so far as they relate to Scotland. There are some restrictions placed upon the power to make subordinate legislation. Such legislation cannot create serious criminal offences, and it is also subject to the same principles of challenge as UK subordinate legislation, for example the *ultra vires* doctrine.

BYELAWS OF LOCAL AUTHORITIES

These are rules made by authorities subordinate to Parliament for the regulation, administration or management of a certain district and/or property. While Parliament makes the broad outline of the byelaw-making power, it is the local authority which then draws up the content and detail of the byelaw. Byelaws are approved by Ministers, not by

Parliament, and they are legally binding on all persons who come within their scope. A common example is the "anti-drinking" byelaw adopted by most Scottish local authorities, which bans the consumption of alcohol within certain public areas.

In Scotland, ss 201–204 of the Local Government (Scotland) Act 1973 deal with the general powers of Scottish local authorities to make byelaws. A local authority may make byelaws for the good rule and government of the whole or any part of its area, and for the prevention and suppression of nuisances therein. Such byelaws must satisfy a number of conditions. They must be within the authority of the authorising statute and must not be contrary to the general law of the land. In addition, they must be certain in their enactment and not unreasonable. Byelaws are capable of being challenged in court as *ultra vires* if they fail to adhere to these conditions and have not been made by following the prescribed procedure.

Byelaws have the same effect as any other law, provided that they are validly enacted. Before being deemed valid, a byelaw must be confirmed by a relevant Scottish Minister. Prior to confirmation, the local authority must inform members of the public of its intention to legislate. This is done by printing a notice in the local newspaper and informing the public of where copies of the draft byelaw can be obtained. This procedure allows citizens to lodge any relevant objections. Such objections must be taken into account by the Scottish Ministers who then have the power to confirm, modify or refuse the byelaw. Once a byelaw has been confirmed, it must be publicised in the area concerned. Local authorities are also obliged to keep a register of byelaws for their area in order to allow public inspection.

Essential Facts

- Subordinate legislation is also known as "delegated" or "secondary" legislation.
- The authority to enact subordinate legislation always comes from an Act of Parliament (known as the "parent" Act).
- The most common examples of subordinate legislation are statutory instruments, Orders in Council and byelaws.
- Acts of the Scottish Parliament may properly be categorised as subordinate legislation.
- Subordinate legislation may not be used for the imposition of taxation.

- It is traditionally unconstitutional to override or alter an Act of Parliament, or any provision of an Act, by way of subordinate legislation. This principle is, however, in jeopardy by virtue of the Legislative and Regulatory Reform Bill.
- *Delegatus non potest delegare* – the principle of sub-delegation applies to subordinate legislation.
- Subordinate legislation must not be retrospective in its effect.
- To remove access to the courts via subordinate legislation is invalid.
- Unlike Acts of Parliament, subordinate legislation is subject to challenge in the courts. Acts of the Scottish Parliament may be challenged utilising the procedure for devolution issues in Sch 6 to the Scotland Act 1998.
- A devolution issue is a question whether an Act of the Scottish Parliament or any provision of an Act of the Scottish Parliament is within the legislative competence of the Parliament.

Essential Cases

Attorney-General *v* Wilts United Dairies (1922): the imposition of taxation by subordinate legislation is unlawful.

Malloch *v* Aberdeen Corporation (1974): subordinate legislation must not be retrospective in operation.

Vine *v* National Dock Labour Board (1957): sub-delegation of subordinate power to another body is unlawful.

Chester *v* Bateson (1920): redress to the courts must not be ousted by subordinate legislation.

A (A Mental Patient) *v* Scottish Ministers (2000): an example of a devolution issue questioning the legislative competence of an Act of the Scottish Parliament.

5 THE *ULTRA VIRES* DOCTRINE

Almost all powers and duties which public bodies possess are conferred by Act of Parliament or statutory instrument (except some arising from the Royal Prerogative, such as treaty-making powers). Thus, the limits of public powers and the extent of public duties are those which statute imposes or grants. The *ultra vires* doctrine is a central principle of administrative law and is a key ground of challenge for judicial review. Generally speaking, the doctrine means that whenever a public body exceeds or misuses its powers it will be acting *ultra vires* (beyond its powers) and unlawfully. In such circumstances, the courts may intervene to correct any wrongdoing.

The doctrine is simple in theory, but fiercely difficult to apply in practice. The more widely expressed a statutory power is, the more difficult it is to decide whether a public body has stepped outside its powers. Thus, the doctrine regularly comes down to issues of statutory interpretation whereby the courts must attempt to place the statutory powers in context and ascertain the true intention of Parliament in affording such powers. These difficulties are further exacerbated by the frequent use of the *ultra vires* doctrine under many narrower and specific categories, such as irrelevant considerations or fettering discretion, all of which ultimately derive from Lord Greene's famous exposition in the case of *Associated Provincial Picture Houses Ltd v Wednesbury Corporation* (1948). These issues are discussed in further detail in Chapter 6.

GENERAL PRESUMPTIONS

In applying the *ultra vires* doctrine, the courts have created certain presumptions, which are universally applicable in the context of administrative law:

(a) The presumption against taxation

Taxation may not be levied without specific parliamentary authority. Thus, a local authority, for example, could not make a charge for something without express power to do so. The classic authority for this principle can be found in *Attorney-General v Wilts United Dairies* (1922), where a 2d a gallon charge levied on milk by the Food Controller was held to be *ultra vires*. The House of Lords found that the New Ministries and

Secretaries Act 1916 gave a wide discretion to the Controller to regulate the supply and consumption of food, but there was no clear provision which allowed for the imposition of such a charge.

(b) Access to the courts must not be denied

In line with the rule of law, the right of citizens to seek redress before the ordinary courts must not be denied without the specific authorisation of Parliament. In *Chester v Bateson* (1920), wartime statutory power was given to a Minister to issue regulations for the safety and defence of the realm. The power was used to issue regulations preventing munitions workers from being evicted from their homes. This prevented landlords from instituting proceedings before the courts for the recovery of property. The regulations were ultimately held to be *ultra vires*, since access to the courts could only be ousted by express statutory authorisation.

(c) Non-retroactivity

Subordinate legislation must not be retrospective in operation. In *Malloch v Aberdeen Corporation* (1974), the Secretary of State for Scotland issued regulations under the Education (Scotland) Act 1962 which stated that every teacher employed by a local authority must be a "registered" teacher. The effect of these regulations was to amend the Schools (Scotland) Act 1956 which provided for school teachers to be "certified". An Aberdeen teacher refused to change from a certificated to a registered teacher and sought declarator that the new regulations were *ultra vires*. It was held that the Secretary of State did not have power to amend the Code so as to take away the vested rights of pre-existing certified teachers. Thus, the amendment of the code was *ultra vires*, at least insofar as it applied to teachers already in employment.

(d) Interference with traditional liberties

The ordinary liberties of the citizen should be interfered with as little as possible. In *McEldowney v Forde* (1971), regulations were issued under the Civil Authorities (Special Powers) (Northern Ireland) Act 1922 which made it a criminal offence to be a member of a "republican club" or "any like organisation howsoever described". McEldowney was charged with being a member of a republican club, but magistrates initially dismissed the charge since there was no evidence of any threat to public order, however, a conviction was ultimately confirmed in the Court of Appeal and upheld by the House of Lords. But Lord Diplock was critical of the regulations and stated that they were too wide to fall within the powers of the 1922 Act. He also said that the intention of Parliament was that the ordinary liberties of the citizen should be interfered with as little as possible, being consistent with the preservation of peace and the maintenance of order. Despite the criticism, it seems that the conviction was upheld in light of the fact that national security considerations were present.

(e) Sub-delegation

When Parliament has given subordinate power to a person or body then power should be exercised only by the person authorised. There is a presumption that sub-delegation to another body is improper, and this is reflected in the Latin maxim *delegatus non potest delegare* – a delegate cannot delegate further. In *Vine v National Dock Labour Board* (1957), the Labour Board had statutory powers relating to discipline which were sub-delegated to a disciplinary committee composed of some of its members. The House of Lords held that disciplinary powers could not be sub-delegated and must be exercised by the body in whom the power was invested. The rule against sub-delegation is not, however, absolute and delegation is possible in certain circumstances, for example where the powers of a Minister are validly executed by individuals within a department.

THE "FAIRLY INCIDENTAL" RULE

The *ultra vires* doctrine can often be unduly restrictive on public bodies and as a result the courts may allow bodies to undertake certain tasks which are otherwise not within their statutory power. This can be achieved by application of the "fairly incidental" rule which was first expounded by Lord Selbourne in *Attorney-General v Great Eastern Railway Co* (1880):

> "the powers of a statutory body ought to be reasonably and not unreasonably understood and applied, and whatsoever may fairly be regarded as incidental to or consequential upon those things which the legislature has authorised ought not (unless expressly prohibited) to be held, by judicial construction, to be *ultra vires*".

In essence, this means that the courts will not only permit bodies to carry out actions expressly authorised but also those which are fairly incidental to their statutory powers. The difficulty, of course, lies in deciding what can be construed as fairly incidental and the rule has been interpreted with varying degrees of flexibility.

In *D & J Nicol v Dundee Harbour Trustees* (1915) the Trustees were a statutory body invested with the function of managing ferries across the River Tay. When the ferries were idle, the Trustees also ran pleasure trips on the Tay. D & J Nicol attempted to stop the Trustees running such trips, on the ground that they were exceeding their statutory powers. Referring to Lord Selbourne's comments in the *Great Eastern Railway Co* decision, the Trustees argued that the pleasure trips were fairly incidental to their express statutory functions. Lord Dunedin, while accepting the principle, held that the pleasure trips could not be construed as incidental and so the actions of the Trustees were *ultra vires*.

A contrasting decision can be found in *Graham v Glasgow Corporation* (1936), where the Corporation decided to set up a printing department to cater for printing, binding and stationery needs. Graham sought to prevent the Corporation setting up such a department, on the ground that it did not have express statutory powers to do so. Although there was no statute which expressly permitted the Corporation to set up a printing department, it did have a wide range of other statutory powers and duties to fulfil. In order to do so, the Corporation required stationery and printing. Thus the court held that creating a printing department was reasonably incidental to the Corporation's statutory functions.

Similarly, in *Attorney-General v Crayford Urban District Council* (1962), the Council had a statutory power of "general management" of council housing. Using this power, arrangements were made with a private insurance company to draw up a cheap insurance scheme for Council tenants to insure their household belongings. A rival insurance company sought declarator that the scheme was *ultra vires*. The Council successfully argued that a prudent landlord would reasonably seek to protect their rent by arranging insurance against the loss of tenants' effects, and so the insurance scheme was fairly incidental to its powers of "general management", and not *ultra vires*.

LOCAL GOVERNMENT AND THE *ULTRA VIRES* RULE

Many of the cases which involve interpretation of the *ultra vires* doctrine concern local government. This is because local government is entirely a "creature of statute" and the powers for its wide and varied functions must be derived from express authority. Indeed, the various activities of local government are governed by a variety of statutes, including Housing Acts, Education Acts, Social Work Acts, Finance Acts and so on. Given the complex legislative foundations of local government, many local authorities have frequently fallen foul of *ultra vires*.

In order to afford some increased liberality to local councils, the Government ultimately embodied the "fairly incidental" rule in statutory form. In Scotland this was achieved through s 69(1) of the Local Government (Scotland) Act 1973 (s 111 of the Local Government Act 1972 for England and Wales). Section 69 (1) provides that:

> "a local authority shall have power to do anything (whether or not involving the expenditure, borrowing or lending of money or the acquisition or disposal of any property or rights) which is calculated to facilitate or is conducive or incidental to the discharge of any of their functions".

However, the introduction of this provision does not allow complete freedom for local authorities to act as they so wish, and challenges may still be brought against actions which cannot be defended by the "fairly incidental" rule.

An example can be seen in *McColl v Strathclyde Regional Council* (1983), where Mrs McColl sought to interdict the Council from adding fluoride to the local water supply with the intention of improving the dental health of the population, especially children. The court held that the Council's statutory duty to provide "wholesome water" in terms of s 6(1) of the Water (Scotland) Act 1980 did not empower the Council to improve dental health, nor could the "fairly incidental" rule be stretched to accommodate such action.

Local Government (Contracts) Act 1997

During the 1980s, the *ultra vires* doctrine caused difficulties in relation to certain financial transactions carried out by local authorities. Many councils entered into speculative schemes known as "interest rate swaps deals" with a view to benefiting from low interest rates. For example, in *Hazell v Hammersmith and Fulham Borough Council* (1992), the Council entered into an interest rate swap contract which involved the lawful borrowing of money from a bank, but then entered into the swap market in order to benefit from lower interest rates. The House of Lords held that such speculation in interest trends was outwith the powers of the Council and could not be interpreted as fairly incidental. Thus the contract was held to be *ultra vires* (see also *Morgan Guaranty Trust Co of New York v Lothian Regional Council* (1995)).

Similarly, many other councils encountered difficulties in attempting to obtain extra finance outwith the statutory rules of borrowing imposed on local authorities. In *Crédit Suisse v Allerdale Borough Council* (1996), the Council established a company to finance a leisure pool and time-share development. Crédit Suisse agreed to provide a loan of £6 million to the company on the proviso that it was underwritten by the

Council. Subsequent sales of the time-share were poor and the Council, being unable to meet the repayments, sought to have the company put into voluntary liquidation. The bank in turn sought repayment of the loan from the authority under the terms of the guarantee. The Council argued that it could not repay the sum as it had no specific statutory power to enter into the contract of guarantee, however, the bank claimed that statutory powers did exist in the form of s 19 of the Local Government (Miscellaneous Provisions) Act 1976 and through s 111 of the Local Government Act 1972.

Ultimately, the Court of Appeal held that neither s 19 nor s 111 gave the requisite authority for a local authority to establish a company underwritten by guarantee to enable it to borrow money. The only implied power under s 111 was one which would allow the authority itself to borrow, and any such power had to be exercised in conformity with other relevant statutory provisions. Thus the use of the company and the provision of the guarantee were *ultra vires* and the contract of guarantee was void and unenforceable (see also *Crédit Suisse v Waltham Forest London Borough Council* (1996)).

In order to deal with the apparent injustice caused to lending institutions and contractors by such decisions, the Government enacted the Local Government (Contracts) Act 1997. Although some recovery from *ultra vires* contracts is possible through the law of restitution in Scotland, the provisions of the 1997 Act also apply to Scottish local authorities. The main purpose of the Act is to provide for a certification scheme whereby contractors can receive an assurance that contracts made with a local authority will not be treated as outwith the powers of the authority or having been improperly entered into. This is without prejudice to any potential challenge to the validity of such a contract by way of judicial review or other proceedings.

Where a certified contract is found to be unlawful by way of judicial review, s 6 of the 1997 Act safeguards any agreed compensation provisions in the contract. Where no such provisions have been agreed, then the local authority will be liable in damages to the contractor. While the Act does address many private-sector fears about contracting with local authorities, it does not provide any real extension of powers for local authorities or abolish the *ultra vires* rule.

A power of general competence?

Despite developments in the law, many within local government still feel that the *ultra vires* doctrine is unduly restrictive. Indeed, the rigidity of the concept was succinctly captured by the Redcliffe-Maud Committee on the Management of Local Government (1967) which felt that *ultra vires* has:

> "a deleterious effect on local government because of the narrowness of the legislation governing local authorities activities. The specific nature of legislation discourages enterprise, handicaps development, robs the community of services which the local authority might render and encourages too rigorous oversight by central government".

In order to deal with the restrictions, the Wheatley Commission on Local Government in Scotland (1969) recommended that local authorities should be afforded a power of general competence, ie a general power to act outwith their statutory powers for the good of the community. However, this proposal was rejected by the Government despite continued calls for the introduction of such a power.

The debate was further fuelled following the creation of the Council of Europe's European Charter of Local Self-Government. The Charter aims to protect and promote local autonomy within Member States and Art 4(2) enshrines the concept of a power of general competence. The Charter was signed by the UK Government in 1997, yet its subsequent ratification proved to be symbolic only, with no real legislative changes being made by the UK Government.

Following the devolution settlement, the Scottish Parliament re-examined the concept of a power of general competence and issued a commitment to fulfil the principles of the European Charter. The McIntosh Commission on Local Government and the Scottish Parliament (1999) recognised that there was widespread support for introducing the power and, following several rounds of consultation, it was encapsulated in the Local Government in Scotland Act 2003. The Act provides for a "power to advance well-being" (the new name for a power of general competence) and is similar in structure to that contained within the European Charter.

The power to advance well-being allows Scottish local authorities to do anything which is likely to promote or advance the well-being of their area and any persons within that area. This includes the power to incur extra expenditure, enter into contractual agreements, facilitate activities and give financial assistance. The power is subject to limits and guidance provided by the Scottish Ministers and it may not be used to duplicate services, raise taxation or override existing statutory provisions which limit local authority powers. If a local authority exceeds its powers, the Scottish Ministers may issue an enforcement direction requiring the authority to remedy the abuse of power. Ultimately, however, the power does not abolish the *ultra vires* rule which still remains as a check and balance in the background.

ULTRA VIRES BY OMISSION

An action by a public body will be *ultra vires* where it does not deal with a matter with which it is expressly or impliedly required to deal. An example can be seen in *Great Portland Estates v Westminster City Council* (1984) where under the Town and Country Planning Act 1971 local authorities had an obligation to draw up a statutory plan setting out proposals for the development and use of land. A plan made by Westminster City Council excluded proposals for office development in the area in question. Instead, the proposals were set out in non-statutory guidelines. This had the effect that people were unable to object to proposals contained in the guidelines. The plan was ultimately held to be *ultra vires* since it did not contain the information which which it was required to deal.

Similarly, in *R v Kirklees Metropolitan Borough Council* (1988) every local education authority had to consider a report from an education committee of the authority before exercising any functions relating to education. The implied purpose of this was to ensure that the authority could benefit from the views of an expert committee. Consequently, each report had to contain an evaluation by the committee of the matter in question, and the detail of the report depended upon the circumstances of each case. In the *Kirklees* case, the Court of Appeal held unanimously that a bare recommendation that a school be should closed down could not constitute a "report". There had to be, at the very least, some explanation of the reasoning behind the recommendations of the report, and since there was none, the actions of the Council were *ultra vires*.

ESSENTIAL FACTS

- The *ultra vires* doctrine is a central principle of administrative law, and is a key ground of challenge under judicial review.
- Most of the powers possessed by public bodies originate from statute, and they must act within the boundaries of those statutory powers. When a public body acts outwith the scope of its statutory powers then it may be acting *ultra vires* (beyond its powers).

- There are a number of general presumptions applicable under the *ultra vires* doctrine which state that certain actions will automatically be *ultra vires* without specific parliamentary authority. These include the introduction of taxation, and attempts to oust the jurisdiction of the courts over citizens.

- *Ultra vires* can often be very restrictive upon public bodies, and so the courts have developed the "fairly incidental" rule to soften its impact. This rule means that the courts will not only permit bodies to carry out actions expressly authorised but also those which are fairly incidental to their statutory powers.

- As "creatures of statute", local authorities have frequently fallen foul of the *ultra vires* doctrine. In an attempt to alleviate their position, various statutory provisions have been enacted. The "fairly incidental" rule has been embodied in s 69 of the Local Government (Scotland) Act 1973, allowing councils to undertake functions incidental to their statutorily authorised ones.

- Recently, local authorities have been given further statutory powers to carry out functions not otherwise authorised which are designed to advance the well-being of their area or citizens. This has been introduced by the Local Government in Scotland Act 2003.

- Despite legislative change, local authorities ultimately remain subject to *ultra vires* as a check and balance in the background.

- *Ultra vires* by omission may arise when a public body has failed to deal with a matter with which it is expressly or impliedly required to deal.

ESSENTIAL CASES

Associated Provincial Picture Houses Ltd *v* Wednesbury Corporation (1948): Lord Greene's statement on the various aspects of misuse of power and *ultra vires*.

Attorney-General *v* Wilts United Dairies (1922): taxation must not be levied without specific parliamentary authority.

Chester *v* Bateson (1920): the right of citizens to seek redress before the ordinary courts must not be removed without parliamentary authority.

Malloch *v* **Aberdeen Corporation (1974)**: subordinate legislation must not be retrospective in operation.

McEldowney *v* **Forde (1971)**: interference with traditional liberties should be kept to a minimum wherever possible.

Attorney-General *v* **Great Eastern Railway Co (1880)**: development of the "fairly incidental" rule.

McColl *v* **Strathclyde Regional Council (1983)**: the "fairly incidental" rule and s 69 of the Local Government (Scotland) Act 1973 in relation to local government.

Morgan Guaranty Trust Co of New York *v* **Lothian Regional Council (1995)**: illegality of "interest rate swap deals" for local authorities.

R *v* **Kirklees Metropolitan Borough Council (1988)**: *ultra vires* by omission.

6 JUDICIAL REVIEW

A cornerstone of administrative law in Scotland is the inherent common law power of the Court of Session to review or supervise acts or omissions of administrative bodies. This is known as the supervisory jurisdiction of the Court of Session, or "judicial review", and the court has had this power since it was first established in 1532. The supervisory jurisdiction was fully expounded by Lord Shaw in *Moss Empires v Assessor for Glasgow* (1917):

> "It is within the jurisdiction of the Court of Session to keep inferior judicatories and administrative bodies right, in the sense of compelling them to keep within the limits of their statutory powers ... but it is not within the power or function of the Court of Session itself to do the work set by the legislator to be performed by those administrative bodies or inferior judicatories themselves."

Thus the Court of Session has the power to ensure that administrative and other bodies act *lawfully*. But since Parliament has entrusted the administrative bodies to carry out certain functions, the court cannot intervene just because a *wrong* decision has been made, or one that the court would not have made. The judicial review process is confined to whether the administrative body's decision was wrong in *law*, not with the *merits* of the decision, as in *Guthrie v Miller* (1827), where, under a local Police Act, commissioners of police were entrusted with the discretion of providing lighting in public streets. Guthrie claimed in the Court of Session that the commissioners were failing in their duty. The question at issue was whether a lamp-post was necessary at a particular spot. The court refused to become involved in the question, on the ground that this would involve deciding whether lamp-posts should be on every street corner. That was a question of *fact* to be decided by the local authority and there was no question of *law* to be judicially reviewed by the court.

SCOPE OF JUDICIAL REVIEW

Unlike in England and Wales, judicial review in Scotland does not favour a strict public/private law approach. As expounded by Lord Hope in the leading decision of *West v Secretary of State for Scotland* (1992):

> "The Court of Session has power, in the exercise of its supervisory jurisdiction, to regulate the process by which decisions are taken by

any person or body to whom a jurisdiction, power or authority has been delegated or entrusted by statute, agreement or any other instrument ... The competency of the application does not depend upon any distinction between public law and private law, nor is it confined to those cases which English law has accepted as amenable to judicial review, nor is it correct in regard to issues about competency to describe judicial review ... as a public law remedy."

This is significantly different from the approach taken by the English courts where the decision on the competency of a review petition is often based upon whether the issue has a sufficient public law element (*O'Reilly v Mackman* (1983)). However, in Scotland, review is not confined to the statutory powers of administrative bodies. It is clear from authority that the supervisory jurisdiction may also extend to the actions and omissions of bodies which are clearly "private" in nature. For example, in *McDonald v Burns* (1940) where the Church expelled two nuns from a convent, and in *St Johnstone FC v Scottish Football Association* (1965) where the SFA fined St Johnstone Football Club. The common characteristic in such cases is not the nature of the body, but the entrusting to it of a decision-making power or duty. This was illustrated by Lord Hope in *West* through his tri-partite relationship which he offers as an indicator for distinguishing reviewable circumstances from those that are purely contractual obligations.

Tri-partite relationship

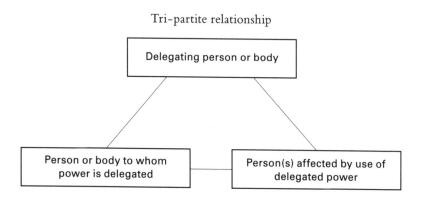

However, Lord Hope's remarks on the tri-partite relationship have been viewed by some as slightly anomalous. In the cases of *Naik v University of Stirling* (1994) and *Joobeen v University of Stirling* (1995), the application of the tri-partite "test" led to markedly different results even when based upon identical facts. In both cases, students had been expelled from

Stirling University for non-payment of fees, yet in *Naik* the circumstances were held to be reviewable while in *Joobeen* they were not. In *Naik*, Lord MacLean considered that there was a tri-partite relationship since powers to discipline students were granted to the University by Royal Charter. He did, however, criticise the tri-partite relationship and was uncomfortable with its use as a "test" in all cases. Conversely, in *Joobeen*, Lord Prosser held that the University was entitled to expel a student for non-payment of fees since this was in essence a contractual relationship and not subject to judicial review.

Due to such confusion, the test has subsequently evolved today into an indicator of the competency of proceedings only in relation to particular disputes concerning contracts and employment matters. It is by no means a test which should be applied in all cases of judicial review and is certainly not a judicial hurdle.

TITLE AND INTEREST TO SUE

It is a general principle of Scots law that litigants must satisfy the Court of Session not only that they are the proper person to pursue the particular proceedings (*entitled*), but also that they have sufficient interest in the outcome of the proceedings. If an applicant fails to satisfy the court on both, this means that there is no dispute between the parties which is capable of being settled by judicial review. The question of title and interest is a separate and logically prior question which must be settled before a case proceeds. The concept was succinctly framed by Lord Dundedin in *D & J Nicol v Dundee Harbour Trustees* (1915): "I think it may fairly be said that for a person to have such a title, he must be a party (using the word in the widest sense) to some legal relation which gives him some right which the person against whom he raises the action either infringes or denies."

In that case, the pursuers were held to have title, not only as harbour ratepayers, but also as electors of the trustees by virtue of Act of Parliament. Similarly, in *Black v Tennant* (1899) Lord Guest held that neighbouring proprietors had title to sue to reduce an invalid grant of a public house licence since they had a statutory right to object to the licensing board on the grant of a licence. Thus, it is clear that title to sue can be created through a statutory relationship. However, where a statute is drawn more specifically, those persons outside its scope will be denied title to sue despite having a sufficient interest, as in Glasgow *Rape Crisis Centre v Home Secretary* (2000) where it was held that the Crisis Centre had no title to sue since the decision of awarding a convicted rapist an entry visa was a matter solely between the Home Secretary and the applicant.

In cases where there is no direct statutory relationship, title to sue can often be based upon a common public right known as an *actio popularis*. This is based upon the principle that some rights are of such a public nature that any member of the public may have title and interest to enforce them. *Actio popularis* has been held to exist in cases relating to public rights of way (*Jenkins v Robertson* (1867)), and rights to use land for recreation (*Home v Young* (1846)). How far public interest extends, however, has been doubted in the case of *Wilson v IBA* (1979) which dealt with the issue of television viewers and electors having the right to enforce a duty against the IBA when it had failed to be politically impartial during a referendum. The question left unanswered in this case was whether any member of the public should have title to sue, or whether a more direct or personal involvement would have to be shown.

The concept of sufficient interest was expounded by Lord Inglis in *Strang v Stewart* (1864) as: "if there be a pecuniary or a patrimonial interest, however small, depending on the determination of the question, the parties have the right to involve the aid of a court of law to resolve their difference".

However, the court has moved away from an insistence on the presence of pecuniary interest, and provided that there is title, interest need be neither pecuniary or large (*Gunstone v Scottish Women's Amateur Athletic Association* (1987)).

Whether a "pressure group" has sufficient interest in the pursuance of the rights of a member of the public has been doubtful under Scots law. In the leading case of *Scottish Old People's Welfare Council, Petrs* (1987), Age Concern Scotland, on behalf of the elderly, challenged the legality of a Government circular which issued guidance on extra payments for severe weather conditions. It was held by Lord Clyde that the interest of the petitioners was too remote. Age Concern was an organisation furthering the interests of elderly people but its own membership did not consist of potential claimants who would directly benefit from a favourable decision. This is a markedly different stance from England and Wales, where pressure groups regularly petition for review on behalf of members of the public (*R v Secretary of State for Trade and Industry, ex parte Greenpeace Ltd* (1998)). Thus, the approach of having sufficient interest in Scotland can often place litigants at a disadvantage. In practice, pressure groups have always been able to fund and provide the means for an individual to raise a petition in Scotland, even if they do not front the actual case.

SUBSTANTIVE GROUNDS OF CHALLENGE

The law relating to the grounds of challenge for judicial review is ever evolving. This is due to the law being based almost wholly upon precedent with very little legislative input. This has allowed the law to develop in a flexible manner, dealing with each case based upon its own unique circumstances. The grounds of challenge have been developed by the courts over many years, however, the most modern authoritative statement on the grounds can be found in the decision of *Council of Civil Service Unions v Minister for Civil Service* (1985). In that case, Lord Diplock set out his famous catalogue of grounds of challenge:

> "one can conveniently classify under three heads the grounds on which administrative action is subject to control by judicial review. The first ground I would call 'illegality', the second 'irrationality', and the third 'procedural impropriety'".

In creating these categories, Lord Diplock did not intend them to be interpreted rigidly. He stated that they would be subject to future expansion and, indeed, he already spoke at this stage about the introduction of a possible fourth ground of challenge in the European principle of "proportionality".

Illegality

Almost all the powers and duties which public bodies possess are statutory, conferred by Act of Parliament or statutory instrument. So the limits of public powers and the extent of public duties are those which statute imposes or grants. Illegality is a central principle of administrative law and can be stated quite simply – a person or body acting under statutory powers can do only those things which statute permits. If a public body exercises its powers without statutory authorisation, then that action will be illegal or *ultra vires* (beyond the powers). The *ultra vires* doctrine is clearly illustrated in *McColl v Strathclyde Regional Council* (1983) where the Council was held to have acted *ultra vires* in attempting to add fluoride to the public water supply. The statutory powers of the Council in this area came from the Water (Scotland) Act 1980 which allowed local authorities to provide a "wholesome" water supply. The court held that the Council's statutory duty to provide "wholesome water" in terms of s 6(1) of the 1980 Act did not empower the Council to improve dental health by adding fluoride; such an action would be illegal or *ultra vires*.

There are a number of other aspects of illegality which are different from the simple application of *ultra vires*. Each of these must be examined in some detail in order to gain a fuller understanding of illegality as a ground of challenge.

Error of law

There is a difference between Scots and English law in the matter of error of law. In England, it is a ground of challenge that an administrative body has made an error of law. Under Scots law, however, the courts have no power to review a decision which is made *intra vires*, even if it involves an error of law (*Don Brothers, Buist & Co Ltd v Scottish National Insurance Commissioners* (1913)). The reasoning for this is that if Parliament has given a body power to deal with certain matters, so, according to theory, Parliament must have intended that the statutory body should not only have the power to make legally correct decisions, but also decisions which go wrong in law.

The leading case is *Watt v Lord Advocate* (1979) where a man had been laid off work for 3 weeks following a work-to-rule in which he had not participated. The issue at stake was whether the man was "directly interested" in the industrial action; if he was, he would not be entitled to unemployment benefit. The case went to the National Insurance Commissioner, who misconstrued the question to be asked – namely whether Watt was "directly interested", and ultimately decided that he was not entitled to unemployment benefit. In the Outer House of the Court of Session, Lord Dunpark stated that there were two possible situations. First, where a decision-maker misapplies statutory words or phrases to the facts of a case and produces a wrong answer, then the court will not be able to intervene. Secondly, where a decision-maker has misconstrued statutory words or phrases which has resulted in the decision-maker exercising a power which they clearly do not have, then the court may intervene by way of review. In the case of Watt, the court refused to intervene, concluding that the decision was in fact within the Commissioner's power, even if it was wrong in law.

On a further appeal, however, the Inner House overturned the decision, holding that the question raised a point of law and that the National Insurance Commissioner had stepped outside his power and acted *ultra vires*. He had not merely misinterpreted the law in attempting to answer the right question; he had in fact misconstrued the law which resulted in him asking the wrong question. But, Lord Emslie did re-affirm the distinction between the two sets of circumstances illustrated by Lord Dunpark in the earlier decision.

Thus, in Scotland, if a body makes an error of law which is not *ultra vires*, the Court of Session will not be able to correct the error. The lack of a remedy is not, however, as important as it might seem, for two reasons. First, from many tribunals and statutory bodies, there is an appeal to the courts provided by statute on a question of law, and, secondly, the courts are likely, as the *Watt* decision perhaps illustrates, to say that any serious error of law takes the decision-making body outwith its power.

Relevant considerations

When an administrative body is entrusted with a power, it is implicit that the power must be exercised taking into account all relevant considerations and excluding irrelevant ones. To say what factors are relevant in any particular case can be difficult, especially when the factors are not expressly laid down in statute. Thus, each case must be judged on its own circumstances.

In *Roberts v Hopwood* (1925), a political decision on sex equality was held to be an irrelevant consideration. Poplar Borough Council had the power to pay its employees "such wages as the council think fit". It decided to pay £4 a week to all employees (including women), which was substantially more than the national average. The District Auditor disallowed this as being contrary to law. On appeal, the House of Lords held that the council had been guided by irrelevant considerations and had used its power for an improper purpose, ie to achieve equality in wages. It had not allowed itself to be guided by relevant considerations such as the cost of living, and wages paid by national bodies and other local authorities.

In *Macfarlane v Glasgow Licensing Board* (1971), the Betting, Gaming and Lotteries Act 1963 stated that a licensing authority could refuse to renew a betting licence on the ground that premises had not been properly conducted. Schedule 4 to the 1963 Act continued to illustrate what constituted proper conduct. In this case, a customer had been refused payment of winnings because the bookmaker had lost the betting slip, and so an objection to the renewal of the licence was lodged. Based upon the objection, the local authority refused renewal. It was held by the sheriff that the non-payment was an irrelevant consideration. It was not one of the matters relating to proper conduct specified in the statute. The Act made clear that relevant considerations were issues such as allowing under-age persons on the premises and restrictions on showing television, none of which had been considered.

A final example of irrelevant considerations can be seen in *R v Ealing London Borough Council, ex parte Times Newspapers* (1986) where the publishers of *The Times* were involved in a bitter industrial dispute with former employees. In response to a call by the trade unions involved,

Ealing Council barred from its libraries all copies of newspapers published by Times Newspapers Ltd. These publications had been part of the library service prior to the ban. The court held that the reason for the ban was that it could be used as a weapon in an industrial dispute. It was therefore not within the Council's powers relating to libraries, and the dispute was an irrelevant consideration.

Improper purpose

A principle of the use of statutory powers is that they must be used for the purpose for which they are granted. This concept is closely related to that of relevant considerations. In *Rossi v Edinburgh Corporation* (1903), ice-cream sellers had to be licensed under statute by the Corporation. The statute in question made it an offence to sell ice-cream outside the hours of 8 am and 11 pm. The Corporation proposed to insert clauses into the licences, to the effect that the premises to which the licence related should not be kept open before 8 am or after 11 pm. The House of Lords held that the clauses were *ultra vires* since the statute did not give the Corporation the power to regulate the opening of shops, only the sale of ice-cream.

Similarly, in *Chertsey Urban District Council v Mixnam's Properties Ltd* (1964), under the Caravan Sites and Control of Development Act 1964, the Council was responsible for licensing caravan sites. They were empowered to impose such conditions as they thought necessary or desirable on the occupier of the land. The Council issued a licence subject to conditions that caravan occupiers should have security of tenure, that there was to be no restriction on the caravaners as to whom they might buy goods from, or on the formation of a tenants" association. All the conditions were subsequently held to be *ultra vires* since the Act was concerned with the licensing of land as a caravan site, and so it permitted conditions which related to the use of the site. It did not permit conditions which attempted to regulate the contracts between the site operator and the caravan occupants.

Improper delegation

The courts hold a presumption that a person or body entrusted with a power should not sub-delegate the exercise of the power to another. This principle is embodied in the Latin maxim *delegatus non potest delegare* – a delegate does not have the power to sub-delegate. This principle is not absolute, however, and delegation may be possible in certain circumstances. In *Vine v National Dock Labour Board* (1957), the House of Lords held that in deciding whether a power to delegate is lawful, one has to consider the nature of the duty in question and the character of the person on whom it is put. In the case of an exercise of disciplinary powers, the House was clear that they could not be delegated.

It is accepted that where powers are granted to a Government Minister, they may be validly exercised by officials of the Minister's department. Only when a statute expressly states that a power must be exercised personally will sub-delegation be unlawful (*Lavender & Son v Minister for Housing and Local Government* (1970)).

Fettering discretion

Often questions can arise as to whether a public authority can limit or restrict the exercise of its own powers – in effect decide that it is not going to exercise its powers. This is known as fettering discretion and may be unlawful.

(1) Fettering discretion by a self-imposed rule. Authorities which have a statutory discretion to do something are entitled to adopt a policy by which the exercise of the discretion will in future be determined. But a body given discretion must not completely disable itself from exercising that discretion. In the leading case of *R v Port of London Authority, ex parte Kynoch* (1919), the Authority had a statutory power to construct docks. Other bodies were also empowered to apply to the Authority for a licence to construct docks. The Authority adopted the policy of not granting a licence for something which was within its own statutory powers of provision and so Kynoch was refused a licence. Lord Justice Bankes held that if a body had passed a rule or come to a decision not to hear any application of a particular nature, no matter who makes it, then this was unlawful. The authority was refusing to exercise a power given to it by Parliament, a power which Parliament must have intended it to use. If, on the other hand, a public body, in the exercise of its discretion, has adopted a general policy but is prepared to consider an application which is contrary to the policy and tells the applicant what the policy is, then, after hearing the application and considering it, it may refuse the application. In such circumstances the exercise of discretion is not wholly excluded even though there is a strong disposition to decide in accordance with the policy.

In *R v Criminal Injuries Compensation Board, ex parte RJC* (1978), the Compensation Board rejected an application based upon the self-imposed rule that a member of a gang injured in a gang fight would not receive an award. This decision was invalidated since, by applying that rule, the Board fettered its discretion and disabled itself from considering on its merits the application of such a gang member, whereas the scheme required every case to be decided on its own merits.

(2) Fettering discretion by agreement or contract. It is clear that an administrative body on which a power is conferred by statute or by common law cannot disable itself by agreement or contract from exercising that power. The leading authority in this area is *Ayr Harbour Trustees v Oswald* (1883). Under the Ayr Harbour Act 1879, the Harbour Trustees had power to acquire land and could use such land for the erection of buildings, among other things. They entered into an agreement with the former owner of a piece of land that they would not obstruct his use of it for access to the harbour, ie they would not erect buildings or otherwise restrict his access. This contract was held to be *ultra vires* in that it fettered their future power to build on that particular land. The power had been conferred by Parliament for the public good and the right to exercise that power should not be restricted in any way.

Similarly, in *Stringer v Minister for Housing and Local Government* (1971), Cheshire County Council made an agreement with Manchester University that it would not permit development which would interfere with the operation of the University's telescope at Jodrell Bank. However, the Town and Country Planning Act 1962 stated that in considering any application for planning permission the planning authority must take into account all material considerations, ie relevant factors. The Council subsequently received an application to build in the area and refused it on the basis of the agreement. It was held that the authority had disabled itself from taking account of all the relevant factors and that the agreement was therefore *ultra vires*.

Irrationality and proportionality

Irrationality, as Lord Diplock expressed in the *Council of Civil Service Unions* case, is to be understood as *Wednesbury* unreasonableness. The concept of *Wednesbury* unreasonableness emanates from the celebrated case of *Associated Provincial Picture Houses Ltd v Wednesbury Corporation* (1948) which did not purport to create new law, but consolidated some already established points. In *Wednesbury*, the Corporation had a statutory power to permit Sunday openings of cinemas "subject to such conditions as the authority thinks fit to impose". Wednesbury gave the plaintiff permission to open, subject to the condition that no children under 15 should be admitted even if accompanied by an adult. The plaintiff sought a declaration from the court that the condition was *ultra vires*. In his judgment, Lord Greene emphasised two points – that the statute had given local authorities an unlimited power to impose conditions, and that it did not provide an appeal from the authority's decision on any ground. He then went on to consider to what extent the decision might be said to be "unreasonable":

> "there may be something so absurd that no sensible person could ever dream that it lay within the powers of the authority. Warrington LJ in *Short v Poole Corporation* gave the example of the red-haired teacher, dismissed because she had red hair. That is unreasonable in one sense. In another sense it is taking into consideration extraneous matters. It is so unreasonable that it might almost be described as being done in bad faith; and in fact all these things run into one another".

In *Wednesbury*, it was quite clear that the subject-matter dealt with by the condition was a matter a reasonable authority would be justified in considering when deciding what condition to attach to the licence. Indeed, the plaintiff did not argue that the council had taken an irrelevant matter into account, but that the decision was unreasonable, treating that as an independent ground of challenge. Lord Greene said even where an authority has observed the relevancy rules, a decision may still be unreasonable when the authority has come to a conclusion so unreasonable that no reasonable decision-maker could ever come to it. However, the threshold of unreasonableness necessary to warrant judicial intervention was, and still is to some extent, pitched at an exceptionally high level. Thus, in returning to the facts before him, Lord Greene said that to prove a case of that kind would require something overwhelming, and in the case of *Wednesbury*, the facts did not come anywhere near the threshold level.

This unusually high threshold reflects the traditional reluctance of the courts to involve themselves in questioning the merits of discretionary decision-making. Indeed, given the constitutional position of the courts, a judge is on dangerous ground in striking down as unreasonable the decision of a statutory authority on a matter given to it for decision by Act of Parliament. This creates a situation whereby the judge substitutes their view on the merits for that of the authority, leading inevitably to claims of *"gouvernement des juges"*.

However, with the arrival of the Human Rights Act 1998, the concept of unreasonableness has undergone a degree of adjustment. In the *Council of Civil Service Unions* case, Lord Diplock referred to the possible acceptance of proportionality into UK law. At this time, proportionality was well established in the jurisprudence of mainland Europe and although absent as a separate ground of challenge under judicial review in the UK, elements of it could be traced in many decisions (*Roberts v Hopwood* (1925); *R v Barnsley Metropolitan Borough Council, ex parte Hook* (1976)). In *R v Ministry of Defence, ex parte Smith* (1996), Lord Bingham stated that:

> "in judging whether the decision-maker has exceeded this margin of appreciation, the human rights context is important. The more substantial the interference with human rights, the more the court will require by way of justification before it is satisfied that the decisions are reasonable".

Thus, the European principle of proportionality has begun to alter the way in which unreasonableness is dealt with by the courts. The introduction of proportionality provides a more rigorous approach to judicial review and involves the court examining the relationship between administrative means and ends. It must examine the level of weight attached by the decision-maker to specific rights and considerations and assess whether the correct balance has been struck. In essence, proportionality is a much less subjective test than that of unreasonableness and attempts to soften the high threshold.

Proportionality should, however, be viewed with caution since it has not replaced the *Wednesbury* standard of unreasonableness but has merely resulted in an adjustment to the law. The test of proportionality is only engaged in cases where Convention and fundamental rights are involved – in all other circumstances, the domestic law remains the same (*R (Association of British Civilian Internees – Far Eastern Region) v Secretary of State for Defence* (2003)). Thus, the concept of proportionality has been incorporated into *Wednesbury* unreasonableness, but for the time being has not replaced it.

Procedural impropriety

In its strict sense, this is a different aspect of *ultra vires* and involves situations where there has been a failure to follow prescribed procedures. This is known as procedural *ultra vires*. However, in a broader sense, procedural impropriety incorporates the rules of natural justice, ie the rule against bias, and the right to a fair hearing. When there has been breach of the rules of natural justice then the courts may interfere with a decision based upon procedural impropriety. The concept of natural justice is dealt with in Chapter 7, therefore this section is restricted to an examination of procedural *ultra vires*.

Legislation relating to the activities of public bodies specifies a great number of procedural requirements. It covers such things as time limits for the service of notices, rights of appeal, and the giving of reasons for decisions, among many others. Where statute lays down statutory requirements, it does not generally specify the consequences that follow from non-compliance, ie it does not generally say whether failure to comply with the legislative procedures invalidates the action or not. Thus, it is almost entirely up to the courts in each case to decide on the issue. However, the courts have shown themselves reluctant to lay down firm rules on this matter and consequently the law has become somewhat fragmented. For example, the fact that a statute uses the word "shall" in relation to certain statutory requirements does not necessarily mean that failure to follow procedure necessarily invalidates the action. Broadly, the courts have to decide whether the requirements are *mandatory* and must be followed, otherwise the action will be invalidated, or *directive*, where failure to follow does not automatically invalidate.

However, this distinction has not been without difficulty and in *London and Clydeside Estates v Aberdeen District Council* (1980), the distinction was held to be too prescriptive by Lord Hailsham who stressed the importance of dealing with each procedural requirement on a case-by-case basis. Consequently, it is difficult to forecast how the courts will treat a particular requirement, but a few generalisations may be made:

(1) If an administrative requirement imposes some financial burden on a citizen, it is likely that the requirement is mandatory and has to be strictly complied with (*Moss Empires v Assessor for Glasgow* (1917)).

(2) If a failure in procedure has an adverse effect on a person's property rights, it is likely that the adherence to the procedure is mandatory (*Eldon Garages Ltd v Kingston-upon-Hull County Borough Council* (1974)).

(3) A failure to comply with a requirement to make an investigation or to carry out a consultation before making a decision that may affect a citizen is likely to invalidate any decision (*Grunwick Processing Laboratories Ltd v ACAS* (1978)).

(4) Where there is a duty to consult, a failure to give those consulted an adequate opportunity to express their views is likely to invalidate a decision (*Lee v Secretary of State for Education and Science* (1968)).

(5) Where a statute gives a right of appeal against a decision, procedures for informing citizens of that right are likely to be mandatory (*London and Clydeside Estates v Aberdeen District Council* (1980)).

REMEDIES

Under Scots law, the three most important remedies are reduction, declarator and interdict. Each of these remedies has been long established, however, a new simplified procedure for their use came into force in 1985 following the recommendations of the Dunpark Committee. Where an application for exercise of the court's supervisory jurisdiction is made, the court may make such order in relation to the offending decision as it sees fit, whether or not such an order was sought in the application; in other words, an application will not fail if it covers one specific remedy but it should have specified another. If appropriate, the correct remedy will be granted. The Court of Session is reasonably flexible, and all three remedies may be sought in the same case, as well as damages.

Reduction

Utilising this remedy, the court may rescind, quash or set aside any written document, including the decision of an inferior court, tribunal or other public body. The grounds of reduction include all grounds which may render the document *ultra vires* (*Palmer v Inverness Hospitals Board* (1963)). Reduction is a very general remedy, but there are a few limitations placed upon its use:

(a) a dismissed employee cannot seek reduction of a notice of dismissal;

(b) reduction will not be permitted if a lesser remedy will suffice (*British Oxygen Co v South-West Scotland Electricity Board* (1956));

(c) reduction is a negative remedy in that another decision cannot be substituted in its place by the court; and

(d) reduction will not be granted if there will be no effect on the position of the parties by virtue of the action (*Shetland Line v Secretary of State for Scotland* (1996)).

A person may seek partial reduction of a decision or part of a document, for example that a condition attached to a licence is *ultra vires*. Partial reduction will only be considered when the offending parts of a document or decision can be appropriately severed from the remainder. In *Darney v Calder District Committee* (1904), a firm of glue manufacturers sought to set up a business in an area where glue production was considered an "offensive business"; thus it obtained a conditional licence. The firm sought reduction of this condition as being *ultra vires*, but it was held that the condition was an inseparable part of the licence so reduction was incompetent.

Declarator

The issue of a declarator involves the court declaring the existence of a right. This can be a right of any kind, for example a question of status, and is not entirely confined to administrative law. It can be obtained in either the Court of Session or the sheriff court, although it should be noted that the sheriff court cannot grant a declarator relating to judicial review (*Brown v Hamilton District Council* (1983)).

The courts will not grant a declarator to settle hypothetical or abstract questions, nor any power entrusted by statute to the exclusive jurisdiction of a specialised tribunal. It may, however, be sought where some future right is in dispute. In *Rossi v Edinburgh Corporation* (1904), Rossi sought a declarator that a proposed licence should not contain prohibitory conditions such as not selling ice-cream on Sundays. The Corporation had not yet tried to enforce the terms of the licence. Rossi could have waited until then, but he chose to take action early to prevent enforcement of the licence; thus a future right was being disputed. The court issued the declarator he sought, namely that to grant a licence subject to such conditions would be *ultra vires*.

However, a declarator will not be granted where it can have no practical effect in settling a dispute. In *Smith & Griffin v Lord Advocate* (1950) the court refused to grant a declarator that Griffin had been a member of the Navy, since the issue in dispute was whether he was entitled to a pension. The court could not grant a declarator because Griffin's pension entitlement was, by virtue of legislation, a matter subject to Ministerial decision. Thus the matter was not within the jurisdiction of the court.

Normally a declarator is accompanied by an action for enforcement of the right declared. In *Baker v Glasgow District Council* (1981), Baker sought a declarator in order to question the legality of a condition in a taxi licence. He also sought an interdict to have the council ordered not to impose the condition.

Interdict

The purpose of an interdict is to prevent injury to or infringement of any right. It is an order of the court prohibiting the implementation of a decision or the continuance of an action and can be sought in a variety of circumstances, for example to prevent the establishing of a local authority printing service (*Graham v Glasgow Corporation* (1936)); to prevent a local authority supporting a political publication (*Meek v Lothian Regional Council* (1983)); and to prevent fluoridation of the public water supply (*McColl v Strathclyde Regional Council* (1983)).

When judicial proceedings are pending, an interim interdict may be granted to maintain the *status quo* until the outcome of those proceedings is known. Whether or not interim interdict is granted will depend on the balance of convenience. In *Innes v Royal Burgh of Kirkcaldy* (1963), the proposal of the Royal Burgh to reduce council house rents by one-quarter was challenged. The court held that the balance of convenience lay in maintaining the existing level of rents, from the point of view that if the reduction was found to be unlawful, tenants would possibly have to find large sums of money to repay the debt.

Interdict is a discretionary remedy. It may be refused even where a proposed action is of doubtful legality, or if there is another competent remedy, such as a statutory penalty or a statutory means of redress. A long delay in taking action or apparent acquiescence in a particular action may lead to an interdict being refused. Interdict may also be excluded when legislation has laid down a system of enforcement, including penalties for breach (*Magistrates of Buckhaven and Methil v Wemyss Coal Co* (1932)).

Remedies provided by statute

When Parliament confers powers and duties upon public authorities it often also provides special procedures for enforcement or appeals or adjudication of disputes. In general, where there is some statutory means of challenging a decision, the Court of Session will require an applicant to resort to that procedure before seeking a remedy; otherwise an action will be dismissed as premature (*Nahar v Strathclyde Regional Council* (1986)). The adoption of this rule is embodied in the principle that the court should not seek to exercise the discretion of another authority or upset the statutory framework for enforcing the law.

The statutory procedures which exist are numerous and there are too many to definitively list. However, examples would include:

(1) the right of appeal by an applicant to the Scottish Ministers on the refusal of a planning permission;

(2) confirmation of local authority byelaws by the Scottish Ministers;

(3) the exercise of a sheriff's powers relating to licensing appeals; and

(4) an appeal from a tribunal to a superior tribunal, such as from an employment tribunal to the Employment Appeal Tribunal.

Essential Facts

- Judicial review is an inherent common law power of the Court of Session in Scotland.
- The judicial review process is confined to whether an administrative body's decision is wrong in *law*, not with the *merits* of a decision.
- The competency of an application for review in Scotland does not depend upon any distinction between public law and private law.
- A potential litigant must satisfy the Court of Session that they have title and interest to sue; if an applicant fails to satisfy the court, this means that there is no dispute which is capable of being settled by judicial review.
- The substantive grounds of challenge under judicial review are illegality, irrationality (or unreasonableness), procedural impropriety and, more recently, proportionality.
- The most common remedies sought under judicial review are reduction, declarator and interdict.

Essential Cases

Moss Empires *v* Assessor for Glasgow (1917): definition of the supervisory jurisdiction.

Guthrie *v* Miller (1827): the distinction between law, facts and merits.

West *v* Secretary of State for Scotland (1992): the scope of judicial review; clarification of public/private law distinction.

Scottish Old People's Welfare Council, Petrs (1987): an outline of title and interest to sue.

Council of Civil Service Unions *v* Minister for Civil Service (1985): an outline of the substantive grounds of challenge under judicial review; the Diplock catalogue.

McColl *v* Strathclyde Regional Council (1983): an example of an action of an administrative body being declared *ultra vires*.

Associated Provincial Picture Houses Ltd *v* Wednesbury Corporation (1948): an explanation of "unreasonableness" and the creation of the high-threshold "*Wednesbury*"-style unreasonableness.

7 NATURAL JUSTICE

One of the most important aspects of modern administrative law is natural justice, or what in more recent cases is referred to as "fairness". The court's right to intervene on the ground of failure to comply with natural justice is based upon the premise that bodies on whom decision-making powers are conferred must act fairly or in accordance with the rules of natural justice. Traditionally, there are two basic rules: the rule against bias (*nemo iudex in causa sua*) and the right to a fair hearing (*audi alteram partem*), both of which will be examined in some detail in this chapter.

There is no simple test as to when the rules of natural justice apply, but there is a tendency for the courts to apply them to all powers of decision-making. In other words, there is a presumption that natural justice will apply (*Gaiman v National Association for Mental Health* (1970)). Historically, the courts used to divide decision-making into three distinct categories: judicial, quasi-judicial and administrative, with natural justice applying to only the former two. However, that position was changed by the decision in *Ridge v Baldwin* (1964) where Lord Reid said that wherever there is legal authority to determine the rights of citizens, there is a duty to act fairly and in accordance with the rules of natural justice. The decision in *Ridge* did not remove all the uncertainties surrounding this area of the law, but it did mark a change in judicial attitudes towards judicial and administrative decisions. In effect, the House of Lords stated that the idea that natural justice only applied to judicial and quasi-judicial decisions was a historical anomaly which was no longer applicable.

The courts today will consider various factors in deciding whether the rules of natural justice apply, with an important overarching factor being the nature of the person or body making the decision. Undoubtedly, the rules of natural justice apply to bodies which resemble courts, for example statutory or disciplinary tribunals (*McDonald v Lanarkshire Fire Brigade Joint Committee* (1959)). But they will also apply in disciplinary proceedings of bodies as varied as trade unions, the Law Society and the General Medical Council, among others. Natural justice will also be generally applicable in circumstances where a body is involved in the determination of an issue between two or more parties. It will therefore apply in connection with such things as planning appeals, compulsory purchase inquiries and inquiries in general.

THE RULE AGAINST BIAS

The first rule of natural justice is that a party must be given an unbiased hearing and decision. This can be further broken down into a number of categories:

Pecuniary interest

Any pecuniary interest, no matter how small, will disqualify a decision-maker. In *Grand National Canal Co v Dimes* (1852), the Lord Chancellor made decisions in favour of a canal company in which he was a shareholder. The House of Lords subsequently set these decisions aside based upon the Lord Chancellor's stakeholder interest. In such circumstances, there is an automatic presumption of bias.

A non-pecuniary interest must be substantial. In *Wildridge v Anderson* (1897) a man was convicted by a magistrate of malicious mischief, for destroying a cushion in a library. It was later discovered that the magistrate was a trustee of the library and therefore an owner of the damaged cushion. Wildridge sought suspension of his conviction, stating that the magistrate was disqualified through bias. In his judgment Lord Moncrieff set out some useful guidelines:

(1) as a general rule, a pecuniary interest, if direct and individual will disqualify, no matter how small;

(2) an interest, though not pecuniary, may also disqualify but it must be substantial;

(3) if an interest is not pecuniary nor substantial and not calculated to cause bias in the mind of the judge, it will be disregarded, especially if to disqualify the judge would cause grave public inconvenience. In such a case, the judge can tell the parties of his interest and ask if they wish him to proceed.

On applying these guidelines, however, Lord Moncrieff stated that the magistrate had no pecuniary interest, nor any appreciable personal interest at all in the case, and was thus not disqualified from the decision-making process.

Similarly, in *Houston v Kerr* (1890), the pursuers argued that a local magistrate who owned a public house in a burgh should be disqualified from considering licence applications for other public houses in the burgh. Despite any interest he may have had in minimising competition for his own public house, he was not disqualified from making decisions. Each case must be decided upon its own merits, but interests other than pecuniary have been held to include among other things membership of an organisation which is a party to proceedings, family ties, professional relationships, partisanship in earlier statements and commercial ties.

Participation

Participation in, or even mere presence at, a hearing by an extraneous person to the proceedings may invalidate a decision. In *Cooper v Wilson* (1937), a police sergeant had been disciplined by his Chief Constable. During an appeal to the Watch Committee against the dismissal, the Chief Constable sat next to the Chairman and was involved in the deliberation of its final decision. The Court of Appeal held that the mere presence of the Chief Constable invalidated the decision since there was a significant risk of bias.

Similarly, in *R v Barnsley Metropolitan Borough Council, ex parte Hook* (1976), a market trader had his licence removed after the market manager reported him to the licensing committee for urinating in a side street. During an appeal against the decision to remove his licence, Hook discovered that the market manager was, at the very least, present while the appeal was being considered. Thus, the decision of the appeal committee was quashed on the ground of bias.

Forming a concluded view

Bias may arise where the deciding party has formed a concluded, as opposed to a provisional, view on the matter. Such a situation would disable the decision-maker from reaching a fair and unbiased conclusion. However, to express views in advance is not usually enough to disqualify a decision-maker (*Bradford v McLeod* (1986)). In *R v Kent Police Authority, ex parte Godden* (1971), a police officer was certified as unfit for duty. When the question of the termination of the officer's employment later arose, the doctor was barred from certifying his medical condition since he had already formed a view on the issue.

Overlapping membership

Complex questions concerning bias may arise when several bodies are involved and there is an overlapping membership. In *Hannam v Bradford City Council* (1970), a teacher had his contract terminated by the school board of governors. Bradford City Council had the power to intervene and stop the dismissal, however, the appropriate committee decided not to exercise this power. Three of the ten members of the committee, including the chairman, were also school governors, though none of them had attended the governors' meeting at which it was decided to terminate the teacher's employment. The Court of Appeal held that a case of bias was clearly present. By being members of the Council committee, the governors did not cease to be an integral part of the body whose action was being challenged, and it made no difference that they did not personally attend the governors' meeting.

Indivisible authorities

In some cases of necessity, the rules of natural justice have to give way when it is impossible to replace a potentially bias decision-maker with and independent one. This can arise when no other person is empowered to make decisions. In *Re Manchester (Ringway Airport) Compulsory Purchase Order* (1935) it was unsuccessfully argued that the only Minister competent to confirm the compulsory purchase order had disqualified himself by showing bias. Though no bias was ultimately found, the courts will not allow statutory machinery to be frustrated in this way by natural justice.

Ministerial or other policy

This is sometimes also known as departmental or administrative bias. It can arise when a Minister has power to make or confirm an order after hearing objections. The Minister's decision cannot be challenged on the ground that he had advocated the order or that he was known to support it as a matter of policy. In *R v Amber Valley District Council, ex parte Jackson* (1984), members of the ruling group on the Council were politically predisposed, as a matter of policy, in favour of a proposed development which required planning permission to be granted. This did not disqualify them or the Council from deciding on the planning application. They were, of course, under a duty to act fairly and to consider all relevant considerations, but there was no evidence to suggest that they would not do so.

THE RIGHT TO A FAIR HEARING

A person who is adversely affected by an administrative decision may argue that the decision was unlawful because they were not afforded the opportunity to put forward a case in their defence. This may include the right to be consulted, to make representations, to submit objections, or to have been "heard" in some other way. There are a variety of aspects to the right to a fair hearing which are best examined individually.

Prior notice

A person who may be penalised as a result of a decision must be given prior notice of the case to answer. This allows an individual to prepare arguments in their defence. In *Cooper v Wandsworth Board* (1863) the Board demolished Cooper's house without giving him a hearing. It was successfully argued that no one should be deprived of his or her property without being given the opportunity to put forward arguments in their favour.

In *Ridge v Baldwin* (1964), a Chief Constable who was dismissed by a local authority Watch Committee was not given notice of the proposal to dismiss him. The dismissal was held to be void since the officer had not been informed of the case he was to meet, nor was he present or given the chance to put forward his own case.

Reasonable notice

Assuming that notice is given of a hearing, then it must be reasonable. In *R v Thames Magistrates' Court, ex parte Polemis* (1974) a shipmaster was accused of dumping oil in the Thames. He was served with a summons at 10.30 am for a hearing at 2 pm the same day. The shipmaster's defence needed time for analysis of the oil, among other things, and received an extension to 4 pm. It was subsequently held that there had been a breach of natural justice as the defence had not received a reasonable opportunity to prepare its case.

Evidence "behind the back"

It is a principle of natural justice that a decision-making body must not take evidence "behind the back" of one of the parties. In other words, it must not take evidence into account without giving both parties a chance to comment upon it. In *Hibernian Property Co v Secretary of State for the Environment* (1973), an inspector of the Department of Environment was holding a public inquiry to decide whether a compulsory purchase order should be upheld in respect of dilapidated housing. After the evidence had been led and the inquiry concluded, the inspector took evidence from residents of the houses who had not spoken at the inquiry. Some of those views were taken into account in the final report which subsequently led the Minister to approve the order. However, the decision was ultimately quashed since the parties to the public inquiry, ie the local authority and the landowners, had not peen permitted to put forward representations based upon the fresh evidence of the residents.

Cross-examination

The rules of natural justice may be breached at an oral hearing where cross-examination of witnesses is not allowed. In the infamous case of *Errington v Wilson* (1995), Errington, the producer of Lanark Blue Cheese, sought judicial review of an order of the local authority calling for the destruction of forty-four batches of cheese. It was alleged that the cheese was contaminated with listeria and so was unfit for human consumption. At the hearing, cross-examination of witnesses was not allowed. It was held that the refusal to permit cross-examination was not in itself necessarily unfair, but where it was clear that there was conflicting evidence, cross-examination was a requirement.

Legal representation

The right to be assisted or represented in the administrative process has been a complex issue. It has been argued that where there is a right to an oral hearing, there is also a right to be legally represented. However, this right has been questioned by the courts. In *Pett v Greyhound Racing Association* (1968), the Racing Association proposed to hold a hearing into the alleged doping of one of Pett's dogs. The Association's procedural rules did not exclude legal representation, therefore Pett asked for a solicitor to be admitted to represent him. However, his request was refused. The Court of Appeal held that Pett did not automatically have the right to be legally represented, citing the fact there was an ultimate right of appeal to the Court, in any event. Lord Justice Lyell stated that he found it "difficult to say that legal representation before a tribunal is an elementary feature of the fair dispensation of justice". Furthermore, the European Convention on Human Rights does not confer an absolute right to legal representation in such circumstances either.

The situation in relation to legal representation has been historically unclear because there has been a desire to avoid the complexity of procedures which legal representation can herald. The expense and delay which can be involved in using such representation could often defeat the advantages of certain administrative tribunals such as benefit appeals. However, it has become clear today that the courts are inclined to accept legal representation as an integral part of justice and fairness, especially where proceedings are judicial in character or involve the potential loss of a person's livelihood. In *R v Leicester City Justices, ex parte Barrow* (1991) Barrow was refused the right to have a friend give him advice and assistance when he was prosecuted for evading the poll tax. His conviction was ultimately quashed when the court held that the concept of fairness should allow a person to seek advice and representation, unless to do so would be contrary to the interests of justice.

Giving of reasons

When no reasons are given for a decision, it can be difficult for an individual to ascertain whether a decision has been diligently made. A decision may have taken into account irrelevant considerations or been subject to an error of law but if no reasons have been given then it may be difficult to challenge the validity of that decision. Despite the importance of giving reasons, there is no general rule under the common law which places an obligation upon decision-makers (*Purdon v City of Glasgow Licensing Board* (1989)). There has, however, been an increasing trend by the courts towards greater insistence on the giving of reasons.

In *Zia v Secretary of State for the Home Department* (1994), a Pakistani citizen married to a British person applied for entry clearance into the UK, but was refused on certain grounds. The applicant was then denied further appeal procedures by the adjudicator and the Immigration Appeal Tribunal, and eventually sought judicial review, arguing that she had been given insufficient reasons. The court held that, in the circumstances, the adjudicator had a duty to give reasons and to make clear what the material considerations in the case were.

Similarly, in *R v Secretary of State for the Home Department, ex parte Doody* (1994), Doody and other prisoners sought to challenge decisions made by the Home Secretary on the lengths of their sentences. The Home Secretary had given no reasons for his decision and, in particular, had not informed them as to whether the judges with whom he was required to consult had recommended a different term from that which he had fixed. It was held by the House of Lords that minimum standards of fairness required that the Home Secretary ought to provide reasons for his decision. Several commentators on this decision considered at the time that *Doody* had created a general duty to give reasons in all cases. However, this was not the case and in fact it merely provides another exception as to the rule that reasons should not be given.

The position was further clarified in *R v Higher Education Funding Council, ex parte Institute of Dental Surgery* (1994), where the Institute wished to challenge the decision of the Funding Council to award it a lower than expected research rating which would result in a funding cut of £270,000. Sedley J held that no reasons were required to be given in this case but he did go on to give guidance on when reasons should be provided. He reiterated that there was no general duty to give reasons for a decision, but accepted that there ought to be certain situations where there is such a duty. One situation is where the subject-matter of a decision deals with a highly regarded fundamental right such as personal liberty or livelihood. In such cases, fairness should dictate that reasons for particular decisions be given as of right. Secondly, where a decision appears grossly aberrant, fairness should require reasons to be given in order that the recipient may assess the aberration legally and decide whether it ought to be challenged.

The giving of reasons must, of course, be complied with where statute provides. In *Brechin Golf and Squash Club v Angus District Licensing Board* (1993), a golf and country club was denied an extension of its Sunday licensing hours, despite this extension having always been granted in previous years. The club asked the board to give reasons for its decision as it was entitled to do so by statute. The board issued a letter detailing its reasons for the refusal, but the club found them to be unsatisfactory, and sought a judicial review. It was held that the reasons were not sufficiently informative to comply with the statutory requirement to give written reasons, and thus the board was ordered to re-consider its decision.

Legitimate expectation

The term "legitimate expectation" was first coined by Lord Denning in *Schmidt v Secretary of State for Home Affairs* (1969) and has since become an important aspect of the right to a fair hearing. Essentially, a legitimate expectation means that an individual will be afforded some protection, for example the right to be consulted, or for an expected procedure or practice to be followed, in a situation where they otherwise have no real legal right. If such an expectation is not afforded, then the individual may seek judicial review. A legitimate expectation may arise from a promise, an undertaking or a regular practice. All are capable of giving rise to an expectation of a kind which the courts will enforce.

In *Attorney-General of Hong Kong v Ng* (1983), the Government announced a policy of repatriating illegal immigrants, stating that each would be interviewed and a decision reached upon individual merits. Ng was interviewed and his removal from the country was ordered. His complaint was that during the interview he had not been allowed to explain the humanitarian grounds on which he might be allowed to stay. He had only been allowed to answer the questions that were put to him. Thus, he had been given a "hearing", but not the kind of fair hearing initially promised. The Judicial Committee of the Privy Council agreed that the Government's promise had not been implemented and so the removal order was quashed. The Privy Council reasoned that Ng had a legitimate expectation that he would be allowed to put his case, arising out of the Government's promise that everyone would be allowed to do so.

A case arising out of the existence of a regular procedure which could reasonably be expected to continue is *Council of Civil Service Unions v Minister for the Civil Service* (1985) where the Prime Minister issued an instruction that civil servants engaged in work for GCHQ, the Government's listening outpost, would no longer be permitted to be members of a trade union. The House of Lords held that the civil servants had a legitimate expectation of consultation before such action was taken as it was well-established practice for the Government to consult before making significant changes to their employees' terms and conditions of service.

Similarly, in *R v Secretary of State for Trade and Industry, ex parte Vardy* (1993), it was held that a decision taken by the Secretary of State to close 31 collieries was illegal, since it was made without any consultation with trade unions. The unions had been deprived of their legitimate expectation that the modified colliery review procedure would be followed, and so the decision to close pits without any independent scrutiny was unreasonable. The modified colliery review procedure was not a legally enforceable procedure, but it gave union members a legitimate expectation that it would be followed.

Essential Facts

- Natural justice is based upon the premise that bodies on whom decision-making powers are conferred must act fairly and justly.
- Traditionally, there are two basic rules of natural justice: (i) the rule against bias (*nemo iudex in causa sua*); and (ii) the right to a fair hearing (*audi alteram partem*).
- The rule against bias ensures that a party is given an unbiased hearing.
- A pecuniary interest, no matter how small, may disqualify a decision-maker as biased; this also applies to a non-pecuniary interest, although this must be substantial.
- Participation in or presence at a hearing by an extraneous person to the proceedings may invalidate a decision by virtue of bias.

- Bias may arise where a decision-maker has formed a concluded, as opposed to a provisional, view on the matter.
- A decision of an administrative body may be unlawful when an aggrieved party has not been afforded the opportunity to put forward a case in their defence. This may include the right to be consulted, to make representations, to submit objections, or to have been "heard" in some other way.
- A person who may be penalised as a result of a decision must be given reasonable prior notice of the case to answer.
- A decision-making body must not take evidence into account without giving both parties a chance to comment upon it.
- The principles of a fair hearing may be breached at an oral hearing when cross-examination of witnesses is not allowed.
- The concept of natural justice should allow a person to seek advice and legal representation, unless to do so would be contrary to the interests of justice.
- There is no general rule under the common law to give reasons for an administrative decision. There has, however, been an increasing trend by the courts towards greater insistence on the giving of reasons.

Essential Cases

Ridge v Baldwin (1964): the scope of natural justice expanded to include administrative decision-making; prior notice of a case – right to a fair hearing.

Grand National Canal Co v Dimes (1852): a pecuniary interest may disqualify a decision-maker under the rule against bias.

Wildridge v Anderson (1897): a non-pecuniary interest must be substantial in order to disqualify a decision-maker.

R v Kent Police Authority, ex parte Godden (1971): forming a concluded view on a matter may disqualify a decision-maker under the rule of bias.

Errington v Wilson (1995): a failure to allow cross-examination of witnesses may offend the right to a fair hearing and invalidate a decision.

Pett v Greyhound Racing Association (1968): the right to legal representation in the administrative process is not absolute.

R *v* **Leicester City Justices, ex parte Barrow (1991)**: the concept of fairness should allow a person to seek advice and representation, unless to do so would be contrary to the interests of justice.

Purdon *v* **City of Glasgow Licensing Board (1989)**: there is no general common law rule requiring decision-makers to give reasons.

Brechin Golf and Squash Club *v* **Angus District Licensing Board (1993)**: reasons for a decision must be given when a statute so dictates.

8 OMBUDSMEN

Not all disputes of an administrative nature have to be resolved in the courts. Indeed, quantitatively speaking, aggrieved citizens are less likely to use the courts than other forms of redress which are readily available to them. This is because access to the courts is still prohibitively expensive for most of the population, except the poor who might qualify for legal aid, and the relatively rich who can afford to instruct their own legal counsel. Those who fall into the "middle income" trap are worse off since they are generally not considered poor enough to qualify for legal aid but neither are they wealthy enough to bear the cost of hefty legal fees. Although moves are being made by the Scottish Executive to reform the legal aid system and allow wider access to justice and the courts for all, there are fortunately many alternative mechanisms for the resolution of administrative disputes.

While there are many informal procedures that can be used, such as complaining to MPs and local councillors, voluntary grievance mechanisms and internal appeals, one of the most powerful means of redress can be found in the system of Parliamentary Ombudsmen. Long regarded as "toothless" and inadequate, the Ombudsmen have in recent years proven themselves to be an invaluable resource for challenging administrative action. The purpose of this chapter is to give an overview of the Parliamentary Ombudsmen in the United Kingdom, namely the Parliamentary Commissioner for Administration (the Westminster Ombudsman) and the Scottish Public Services Ombudsman (the Scottish Ombudsman).

THE PARLIAMENTARY COMMISSIONER FOR ADMINISTRATION

Introduction

Since the early 19th century, Scandinavian countries have had an official, known as the Ombudsman, whose function is to investigate the grievances of ordinary citizens. The word "ombudsman" itself is Norse in origin and means "commissioner". The appointment of such a commissioner in the United Kingdom is comparatively recent, dating from the Parliamentary Commissioner for Administration Act 1967. Previously, complaints against government departments would be pursued, either by complaining to an MP or by seeking judicial review.

Both of these mechanisms are, of course, limited since MPs cannot mount a very effective investigation into the working of government departments, and largely have to limit themselves to asking questions of Ministers in the House of Commons, while judicial review can be invoked only by those with title and interest to sue and is limited to reviewing the legality of the actions.

To address these issues, the Whyatt Report on *The Citizen and Administration* (1961) advocated the creation of an Ombudsman as adopted in the Scandinavian countries. The primary aim of the Ombudsman would be to investigate complaints of maladministration in central government departments. Despite considerable opposition to the concept, the Ombudsman was created by virtue of the Parliamentary Commissioner for Administration Act 1967.

Constitution, appointment and tenure

The Parliamentary Commissioner for Administration Act 1967 establishes the office of the Parliamentary Commissioner for Administration (PCA), commonly known as the Westminster Ombudsman. The independence of the PCA from the executive is protected and the 1967 Act affords a degree of security of tenure. The PCA is appointed by the Crown on the advice of the Prime Minister and holds office during good behaviour, subject to a power of removal on address from both Houses of Parliament. Thus, the tenure is similar to that of a High Court judge. The PCA also has a salary fixed by statute which is chargeable to the Consolidated Fund and the office carries its own staff, subject to Treasury approval as to numbers and conditions of service.

Jurisdiction

The primary function of the PCA is to investigate complaints by private citizens that they have suffered injustice as a result of maladministration by government departments, agencies and non-departmental bodies. The full list of bodies subject to the jurisdiction of the PCA is listed in Sch 2 to the 1967 Act and includes all major government departments as well as other non-departmental bodies such as the Arts Council and the Equal Opportunities Commission. As regards those departments subject to investigation, the PCA cannot investigate complaints relating to the exercise of legislative functions, such as the preparation or creation of delegated legislation, although he can investigate complaints into the way in which a scheme set up by way of delegated legislation is actually being administered.

There are also a number of areas which are outwith the Ombudsman's jurisdiction. These can be found in Sch 3 to the 1967 Act and include, *inter alia*, matters certified by a Secretary of State to affect relations between the UK Government and any other government or international organisation; the commencement of civil or criminal proceedings before any court of law in the UK; action taken in matters relating to contractual or other commercial transactions of government; and action taken in respect of any personnel matters. The 1967 Act also states that the PCA may not investigate a matter where the citizen generally has a right of redress before any tribunal or court.

As mentioned above, the Ombudsman can only investigate instances of maladministration causing injustice. However, the term "mal-administration" is not defined anywhere within the 1967 Act. This has often been criticised by observers of the system. However, this was a deliberate act of the legislature and has allowed the concept to develop unrestricted, on a case-by-case basis. In the Second Reading debate on the Bill, Richard Crossman MP famously catalogued possible examples of maladministration as bias, neglect, inattention, delay, incompetence, ineptitude, perversity, turpitude and arbitrariness. Its definition is wide and encompassing, however, it does not generally include the merits of a decision and there must always be an element of injustice present.

Making a complaint

The PCA cannot instigate an investigation personally but can only respond to complaints received from members of the public. Currently, the PCA is only entitled to investigate complaints made in writing by a Member of the House of Commons at the instance of a member of the public. The public have no direct access to the PCA and must first approach an MP and request that the complaint be forwarded in writing to the Commissioner. The MP may, of course, refuse. This is known as the "MP filter" and is intended to serve three functions. First, it acknowledges the status of the Commissioner as a servant of Parliament; secondly, it provides the MP with an opportunity to deal with the complaint as they see fit; and finally, it allows inappropriate and vexatious complaints to be rejected before reaching the PCA, thus reducing workload.

The MP filter has been much criticised and the UK and France are the only two European countries which have such a filter. The arguments in favour of the MP are not particularly convincing and, in any event, most MPs have today adopted a policy of always referring complaints to the PCA as they are reluctant to reject them for fear of appearing unhelpful to constituents. Thus, the filter provides no real practical purpose. The Parliamentary Commissioner (Amendment) Bill was introduced into the House of Commons on 15 February 2000, with the intention of removing the MP filter and to allow the PCA to investigate complaints received directly from members of the public. However, this was a Private Member's Bill and failed to progress through Parliament. Given that the Scottish Parliamentary Ombudsman has no filter, it is likely that there will be a further attempt at abolition in the near future.

Complaints must also be made within 12 months of the date on which the citizen first had notice of the issue complained of. This is subject to a discretionary power to allow late applications in extraordinary circumstances.

Investigations

If a complaint does fall within the jurisdiction of the Commissioner then an investigation may be conducted. At this primary stage, the PCA should try to promote an amicable settlement between the individual and the department or body concerned. However, if this is not possible then an investigation will proceed in accordance with the 1967 Act. All investigations are conducted in private, and the department or body complained of must be given an opportunity to comment on any allegations contained in the complaint. The PCA has powers similar to those of a High Court judge for securing the presence of witnesses and the production of documents, and Crown privilege or public interest immunity cannot be used to exempt information from investigation by the Commissioner.

The PCA is protected in the conduct of investigations by the laws relating to contempt of court and so any wilful obstruction of an investigation may be punished as if it were a contempt. Complainants and witnesses who have spent time in assisting an investigation are entitled to claim reasonable expenses.

Reports

On completing an investigation, the PCA must issue a report of the findings to the MP who originally referred the complaint, and to the department or body against whom the complaint was made. If the report finds that injustice was caused by maladministration and this has not been rectified by the department or body concerned, then he may lay a further special report before both Houses of Parliament. The Commissioner may also make other special reports as are necessary and must make an annual report to Parliament. The reports of the

Commissioner and certain other information relating to investigations are absolutely privileged in the law of defamation.

Enforcement

The PCA cannot have any recommendations or reports enforced by law. The Commissioner has no executive power and cannot alter decisions made or order payment of compensation. If, after conducting an investigation, the Commissioner considers that an injustice has not or will not be remedied then he or she may lay before each House of Parliament a special report on the case recommending remedial action. That is, however, the extent of the PCA's powers. The issue must then be left to the doctrine of ministerial responsibility, the assumption being that pressure will be put upon the Minister concerned to take remedial action. This may not seem like a particularly strong method of enforcement, however, in reality there is strong pressure on the Government to comply with the PCA's findings. Such special powers are often not necessary, since an agreed settlement involving, for example, an apology or compensation, may be reached between the aggrieved individual and the government department concerned.

Reform

Today, there is less in the way of criticism of the PCA and more in the way of concern about the workload of the Commissioner. Over the last decade or so, the PCA's total workload has increased from 801 complaints in 1991 to 4,189 complaints in 2005. Furthermore, up until 2002, the Parliamentary Commissioner also held the offices of Scottish Parliamentary Commissioner for Administration, and Health Service Commissioner for England, Scotland, and Wales: a particularly burdensome remit, fuelling the rise in complaints.

The high instance of complaints would seem to suggest that the PCA is a highly successful and efficient body. However, the system has recently come under intense public and parliamentary scrutiny. Much of the criticism arising from this has not necessarily been directed solely at the PCA but more at the lack of uniformity across the Ombudsmen system. Besides the PCA, there are several other public- and private-sector Ombudsmen in England and Wales, for example the Commissioner for Local Administration (dealing with local government), and the Legal Services Ombudsman. Each of these Ombudsmen has separate remits with differing powers and procedures, with the result that it can often be confusing for a citizen to know exactly where to direct complaints.

Consequently, the Cabinet Office has published a review of the system, entitled *Review of the Public Sector Ombudsmen in England* (2000). This paper has been well received but it has yet to elicit any major legislative change. Among its key proposals, the paper suggests having a collegiate Ombudsmen system with a direct point of access for citizens. This would introduce a more uniform approach and would make the system more accessible at the point of use for aggrieved citizens. Such change would, however, have to take into account the already pressurised resources of the existing system.

SCOTTISH PUBLIC SERVICES OMBUDSMAN

Introduction

The creation of the Scottish Parliament has led to the inception of a modern Ombudsman system in Scotland. Section 91 of the Scotland Act 1998 placed an obligation upon the Scottish Parliament to create an Ombudsman (or to make alternative arrangements) to deal with any complaints of maladministration in devolved areas. Thus, from July 1999 until 2002, complaints against the Scottish Executive, the Scottish Administration and other public bodies in Scotland were handled by the Westminster Ombudsman in his role as Scottish Parliamentary Commissioner for Administration. This interim period allowed the Scottish Parliament to hold a series of consultations in order to canvass opinion as to the best mechanism for handling complaints within Scotland.

The result of this consultation was the Scottish Public Services Ombudsman Act 2002 which has established a modern collegiate approach to complaint handling in Scotland. Under the 2002 Act, the various Scottish public-sector Ombudsmen have been amalgamated into one centralised body, allowing for ease of use and simplicity. Although the strengths of the separate Ombudsmen were widely recognised, the disparity between the offices was frequently confusing for members of the public. The new "one-stop shop" approach allows the Ombudsman system to become more co-ordinated and centralised.

Constitution, appointment and tenure

Under the 2002 Act, the new Scottish Ombudsman has assumed the jurisdiction of the transitional post held by the PCA, although the PCA may still investigate maladministration within reserved areas of government. The Scottish Ombudsman has also assumed the jurisdiction of other pre-existing ombudsmen in Scotland, namely the Commissioner for Local Administration in Scotland, the Health Service Commissioner for Scotland, the Housing Association Ombudsman for Scotland, the External Adjudicators for Scottish Enterprise and Highlands and Islands Enterprise, and the Mental Welfare Commission.

The Scottish Ombudsman is appointed by the Queen on the nomination of the Scottish Parliament, and is assisted by three Deputy Ombudsmen who are similarly appointed. The Deputy Ombudsmen are intended to reflect the expertise held by former office holders and to this end the current Deputies are drawn from the fields of health, housing and local government.

The Ombudsman and any Deputy Ombudsman may hold office for a period not exceeding 5 years, subject to a power of removal in pursuance of a resolution of the Scottish Parliament. Office holders are eligible for reappointment but may not serve a third consecutive term unless through special circumstances it is in the public interest for them to do so. In any event, any office holder who attains the age of 65 must vacate office on 31 December of that year.

The Ombudsman and any Deputy Ombudsman have a salary fixed by the Parliamentary Corporation and the office also carries its own staff, subject to approval as to numbers and conditions of service.

Jurisdiction

The primary role of the Scottish Ombudsman is to investigate complaints from members of the public who claim to have suffered injustice or hardship as a consequence of maladministration by the Scottish Government, agencies and other non-departmental bodies. Schedule 2 to the 2002 Act provides a full list of bodies subject to the jurisdiction of the Ombudsman and is split into two Parts. Part 1 contains a list of authorities which cannot be amended and includes members of the Scottish Executive, health service bodies, local authorities and the police, among others. Part 2 contains a list of Scottish public authorities and cross-border public authorities such as Scottish Enterprise, the Scottish Legal Aid Board and the National Consumer Council. This list may be amended in the future by Order in Council.

With regard to those bodies subject to investigation, there are a number of restrictions placed upon the jurisdiction of the Ombudsman. Schedule 4 to the 2002 Act excludes 15 categories of investigation; these include action taken for the prevention of crime, any civil or criminal legal proceedings, action taken which relates to contractual or commercial matters, action takes in respect of any personnel matters and any decision made in a judicial capacity. Furthermore, the Ombudsman may not question the merits of discretionary decisions unless there has clearly been maladministration nor may any matter be investigated where the complainant has an alternative remedy available, for example a right of appeal.

As with the PCA, the concept of maladministration has no direct statutory definition, in order to allow flexibility. But there have been criticisms of the Scottish Ombudsman in that s 5 of the 2002 Act includes alongside maladministration the right to investigate "service failures" and "any action" (where the action is taken by a registered social landlord, or a health or family care provider). Thus, s 5 essentially provides additional grounds of investigation which are exercisable only in very specific circumstances. This is somewhat at odds with the centralised ethos of the 2002 Act and may add unwarranted confusion for users of the system. In response, the Scottish Parliament has defended the disparities, claiming that they are necessary to reflect the procedural nuances of the pre-existing Ombudsmen.

Making a complaint

An innovation of the 2002 Act can be found in the removal of the "MP filter" concept, resulting in the absence of an "MSP filter" for Scotland. Thus, in keeping with the spirit of a collegiate approach, citizens may complain directly to the Scottish Ombudsman. It is also possible to have a complaint lodged on a person's behalf by any authorised person, for example an MSP or a local councillor. As with the PCA, complaints must be made within 12 months of the date on which the citizen first had notice of the issue complained of, subject to a discretionary power to allow late applications in extraordinary circumstances.

Complaints may be submitted either in writing or electronically. This is a key difference from the procedure followed by the PCA where all complaints must be submitted in writing. Although the vast majority of complaints are generally written, there is a growing sector of the public who prefer to deal with issues via the Internet. As a result, citizens may submit complaints using an electronic submission form available on the Ombudsman's website. The Ombudsman also has a discretionary power to accept oral complaints in extraordinary circumstances.

Investigations

If a complaint falls within the jurisdiction of the Ombudsman then an investigation may be conducted. The procedure for investigation is very similar to that of the PCA and is in fact modelled closely upon the 1967 Act. Investigations are conducted in private, and the department or body complained of must be given an opportunity to comment on any allegations contained in the complaint. The Ombudsman may compel the production of any information or documents required and has similar powers to those of a Court of Session judge for securing the presence and examination of witnesses. Crown privilege or public interest immunity claims cannot be used in relation to documents subject to investigation by the Ombudsman.

Reports

On completing an investigation, the Ombudsman must report the findings to the complainant; the department, body or person against whom the complaint was made; and the Scottish Ministers. Furthermore, a report must be laid before the Scottish Parliament which must not identify any person other than the department, body or person complained of. If the Ombudsman finds that hardship or injustice has been caused by maladministration and this has not been rectified then a special report may be laid before the Parliament. In addition, the Ombudsman must also present an annual report to the Parliament.

Enforcement

As with the PCA, the Scottish Ombudsman cannot have any recommendations or reports enforced by law. The Ombudsman has no executive power and cannot alter decisions made or order pay-ment of compensation. If, after conducting an investigation, the Ombudsman considers that an injustice has not or will not be remedied then a special report on the case is the strongest form of action. Enforcement is left up to ministerial responsibility and the assumption that pressure will be put upon the Government to take remedial action. This may not seem like a particularly strong method of enforcement for a modern Ombudsman system. However, the Scottish Executive identified that keeping enforcement powers to a minimum would in fact aid co-operation between bodies and the Scottish Ombudsman, whereas investing draconian powers of intervention would be likely to hinder investigations. To date, the Scottish Executive appears to have been correct and many cases have been settled through apology, compensation or remedial action stemming from the Ombudsman's comments.

FURTHER REFORM

The concept of maladministration

Maladministration as a ground of referral has frequently been criticised as too narrow and can be contrasted with the position of the New Zealand Ombudsman who may investigate any decision or act which appears to be "wrong". It was suggested by the 1977 Justice Report *Our Fettered Ombudsman* that maladministration be replaced with the phrase "unreasonable, unjust or oppressive", but this change has never materialised. Conversely, it can be argued that the concept of maladministration is not in fact narrow, and that it might well be possible to challenge unreasonable, unjust or oppressive actions by claiming that they are the result of ineptitude or arbitrariness on the part of government officials. A previous Commissioner, Sir Idwal Pugh, stated publicly that he regarded his work as being concerned with just such unreasonable, unjust or oppressive actions, and he would have no hesitation in concluding that there must have been some aspect of maladministration in the procedure leading to the taking of such a decision. The courts have not insisted that the complaint must indicate what aspects of maladministration are alleged. The application merely needs to indicate what the complaint is about, leaving it to the Ombudsmen to discover any maladministration. This approach can be seen in *R v Local Commissioner for Administration for the North and East Area of England, ex parte Bradford City Council* (1979).

However, the concept of maladministration is certainly confusing. This is especially true of the Scottish Ombudsman, where an investigation may go beyond maladministration into service failures and other actions, but only in limited circumstances. This may be likely to result in the less socially confident, and less articulate, being able to understand the nature of any complaint.

Inadequate use of press and publicity

It has often been stressed that the Ombudsmen should make more extensive use of the Press, by supplying full details of all reports. Traditionally, reviews and comment upon the reports appear in various specialised journals but general public awareness of the system is low. Greater publication of reports would also bring extra pressure to bear on the Government to correct any injustice uncovered. To date, the Ombudsmen have not utilised any greatly increased amount of publicity, however, they have attempted to be more accessible and user-friendly. This has been achieved chiefly through information technology and the creation of user-friendly websites providing a portal for initial complainants. The website of the PCA can be accessed at www.ombudsman.org.uk, and that of the Scottish Ombudsman at www.scottishombudsman.org.uk.

Jurisdiction

The Ombudsmen cannot carry out an investigation where the act in question has been carried out in accordance with law and without maladministration. This is the case even though the law in question is operating in an unfair, unreasonable, oppressive or unintended way. Indeed, it may be that the fault is not with a government department or body but with the legislation that it is obliged to execute. The question thus arises as to whether Ombudsmen should be able to investigate such instances and have the power to suggest changes in legislation, including statutory instruments. This would be beneficial to Parliament since the Ombudsmen are ideally placed to form a view as to whether current legislation is working in an undesirable way on the ground.

Essential Facts

- The Parliamentary Commissioner for Administration (PCA) was created by the Parliamentary Commissioner for Administration Act 1967 which lays out the composition, jurisdiction and powers of the PCA. The remit of the PCA extends to England and Wales, as well as any reserved matters for Scotland.

- The primary role of the PCA is to investigate complaints by private citizens who have suffered injustice as a result of maladministration by government departments, agencies and non-departmental bodies. Complaints must be made in writing and initially through an MP; this is known as the "MP filter" and has been much criticised.

- The Scottish Public Services Ombudsman (SPSO) was created by the Scottish Public Services Ombudsmen Act 2002 which lays out the composition, jurisdiction and powers of the SPSO.

- The SPSO is a collegiate body and also incorporates the jurisdiction of pre-existing ombudsmen in Scotland, namely the Commissioner for Local Administration in Scotland, the Health Service Commissioner for Scotland, the Housing Association Ombudsman for Scotland, the External Adjudicators for Scottish Enterprise and Highlands and Islands Enterprise, and the Mental Welfare Commission.

- The primary role of the SPSO is to investigate complaints from members of the public who have suffered injustice or hardship as a consequence of maladministration. Complaints may be made directly to the Ombudsman since there is no "MSP filter".

- Both the PCA and the SPSO have the power to conduct investigations into instances of maladministration and have statutory authority to compel the production of documents and witnesses.

- On completion of an investigation, the PCA must produce a report containing findings and recommendations and may lay a special report before Parliament where no remedial action is taken in light of the report. The SPSO must act similarly, with a special report being laid ultimately before the Scottish Parliament.

- Neither the PCA nor the SPSO has any legal powers of enforcement. They cannot coerce action to be taken in light of their recommendations. Instead, they rely upon co-operation from bodies complained of through ministerial responsibility and Government pressure.

9 TRIBUNALS AND INQUIRIES

From the Second World War onwards, the size and complexity of the Welfare State in the UK have grown tremendously. Consequently, the state has become involved in more areas of everyday life than ever before. This has led to a marked increase in the number of complaints and disputes which arise from the application of rules and regulations by various organs of the state. These disputes could be settled using the existing courts. However, the court system already struggles to cope with ever-increasing litigation in other areas. As a result, Parliament decided to create special bodies, known as "tribunals", for resolving certain categories of dispute between citizens and the state. It also created a number of tribunals with jurisdiction over disputes between citizens, for example in the area of employment law.

As with many other features of administrative law in the UK, tribunals have emerged in a patchwork fashion, with little real thought being given to their theory or general principles. The essential feature of tribunals is that they are bodies which are distinctly separate from the court structure, and are independent of government departments. Most tribunals are set up by statute and the powers and scope of the tribunal are contained either within the statute or in regulations issued under its authority. They have a limited scope of authority to deal with administrative-type issues, which are often, but not necessarily, disputes between public authorities and citizens. There are many types of tribunal in the UK today and they cover a wide range of disputes including immigration appeals, employment tribunals, disability living allowance tribunals, benefit appeals and criminal injuries compensation, among many others.

The position of tribunals within the justice system was clarified in 1958 by the Franks Committee (*Report of the Committee on Administrative Tribunals and Inquiries* (1957)) and the recommendations of the Committee were embodied in the Tribunals and Inquiries Act 1958, now consolidated in the Tribunals and Inquiries Act 1992. The Franks Report was instrumental in the development of the modern tribunal system and stated that all tribunals should be open, fair and impartial, meaning that they should be free from Government interference, have clear and consistent procedures, and should be held in public, giving clear and reasoned decisions.

WHY USE TRIBUNALS?

Obviously, the types of issues dealt with by tribunals could alternatively be decided by a Government Minister or department, or by the courts. However, there are a number of key reasons why tribunals are used:

(1) Tribunals are preferable to a ministerial decision since they are not influenced by policy in the same way that a Minister would be. Tribunals have a body of statutory rules and codes which they must follow and their task is generally to decide whether, in terms of the rules, an individual making a claim is entitled to succeed. In this way, the tribunal system resembles that of the courts in that it is concerned with the application of statutory rules and not policy. The fact that decisions are made by a separate body leads to increased public confidence.

(2) Tribunals are preferable to courts because of their cheapness and speed. Courts are generally slow and expensive and are inappropriate for many types of administrative disputes. The ordinary courts are in essence a "jack of all trades" and have a very wide jurisdiction. For example, Court of Session judges can be dealing with divorce one day and contractual disputes the next. Consequently, it is unrealistic to expect judges, who are in effect general practitioners, to have the necessary expertise and familiarity to deal with the complex issues of tribunals. Many of the statutory schemes which tribunals have to interpret are very complex and decision-makers can only become expert by intensive specialisation.

Thus, tribunals which handle only cases of one particular type can easily become expert in specific areas and recruit members who have specialist knowledge. An example of this can be found in the Lands Tribunal for Scotland, which decides questions of compensation for land which is the subject of compulsory purchase orders. In dealing with such issues, difficult legal and valuation questions frequently arise. The chair of the Lands Tribunal must be a lawyer but always sits with at least one other member, who will be an expert valuer or surveyor who can handle any technical question that arise.

(3) If all disputes were dealt with by the courts, there would have to be an enormous increase in the number of judges, since the court system is already overburdened. The Franks Committee suggested that this would inevitably lower the quality of judges

and concluded that the system of administrative tribunals had, in this way, positively contributed to the preservation of the ordinary judicial system.

(4) Tribunals are more user-friendly than the courts. The court system is designed by lawyers for use by lawyers and as such is very formal. Ordinary citizens are often intimidated by the adversarial approach of courts and do not feel at ease in them. Rules of procedure and evidence are complex and as a result many feel the need to employ a lawyer to conduct their case. Tribunals, on the other hand, are generally more informal, and do not operate the same rigid procedural rules. Tribunals are generally inquisitorial in procedure and the informality allows an individual to represent themselves.

(5) Tribunals can be more aware of the social implications of the statutory scheme which they have to operate. Many judges take a strict, literal approach to statutory interpretation, and are as a result reluctant to consider the underlying purpose of the legislation. Tribunal members, on the other hand, may well take a more sympathetic approach.

(6) Tribunals can allow a greater degree of flexibility than the courts. There is often an overwhelming desire for certainty on the part of the courts as they strive to adhere to the rules of precedent. Although there is much to be said for this, rigid legal rules can often develop. However, tribunals are free from the restrictions of the courts and often take a much more flexible approach. As a result, they have a lesser tendency to lay out hard and fast legal rules.

COUNCIL ON TRIBUNALS

One of the most important recommendations of the Franks Committee was that a Council on Tribunals should be established, to act as a supervisory body for the tribunal system. Franks suggested that there should be two separate Councils on Tribunals: one for England and Wales and one for Scotland. However, the Government ultimately set up only one, albeit with a separate Scottish Committee. The Council consists of 10 to 15 members and a salaried chair appointed by the Lord Chancellor and the Lord Advocate. The Scottish Committee has two or three members of the full Council plus three or four non-members of the Council appointed by the Lord Advocate. The Council has a number of key functions:

(1) to keep under review the constitution and workings of the tribunals;

(2) to make recommendations to the appropriate Minister about the appointment of members of tribunals;

(3) to be consulted by the Minister on procedural rules for tribunals;

(4) to be consulted by Ministers prior to a decision to exempt a tribunal from the duty to give reasons; and

(5) to consider and report on such matters as are referred to it by the Lord Chancellor or Scottish Ministers with regard to tribunals.

The Council is merely an advisory and consultative body, with no decision-making functions. It has no power to investigate complaints from members of the public and is unable to initiate investigations unless they relate to the constitution and working of tribunals. Council members pay occasional visits to tribunals and observe and report on their operation. Members' reports are confidential and not made open to the tribunals.

The Council is often criticised as being ineffective, but this is almost wholly becuase of under-funding, under-staffing and a relatively poor political position. It must be consulted by government departments before procedural rules are made for tribunals, but its advice need not be taken or even referred to.

CONSTITUTION OF TRIBUNALS

Members

Traditional tribunals have a panel consisting of three members, namely a legally qualified chair and two "wing" members. The wing members generally consist of an expert and a layperson with relevant experience (eg in mental health or disability). They will tend to be bias towards their own side but bring invaluable knowledge and experience to the tribunal. Many steps have been taken over the years to ensure the independence of tribunal members. Traditionally, tribunals have been set up under the auspices of government departments and so Ministers have regularly been directly involved in the appointment of members. The Franks Committee recommended that this practice should have been replaced whereby the Lord Chancellor (or the Lord Advocate in Scotland) and the Council on Tribunals would directly appoint all members. However, this has not been reflected in subsequent legislation and under the Tribunals and Inquiries Act 1992 both the Lord Chancellor and the relevant Minister may formally appoint members while the Council may only make recommendations.

Procedure

Prior to the Franks Report, there were striking differences between the procedures followed in different tribunals. There were no generally applicable rules to such things as legal representation, openness of hearings and the giving of reasons. Franks highlighted the need for consistency among tribunals and many of his recommendations can now be seen in the 1992 Act.

Pre-hearing

With regard to procedure prior to a hearing, Franks insisted that legal advice should be made available under an official scheme. This would allow citizens to know in advance the nature of the case they would have to meet. This is standard practice today, and is covered by individual tribunals' rules. It is not an overly formalised procedure and often involves the citizen receiving a document setting out the main points of the other side beforehand.

Procedural rules

In relation to the procedure used during hearings, the Franks Committee thought it important to preserve informality while at the same time maintaining an orderly procedure. Franks thought procedure was of the utmost importance, and should be clearly laid down in statute or statutory instruments. However, since tribunals are so diverse in their subject-matter, it would not be appropriate to rely on a single or small number of procedural codes covering all tribunals. As such, tribunals have a discretion in producing their own rules of procedure. They may vary procedures where it seems necessary in the interests of justice but all tribunal rules must be produced in consultation with the Council on Tribunals, which can advise on best practice. Despite the existence of such rules, actual procedure is largely at the discretion of the chair.

Openness

It is a fundamental principle of tribunals that hearings be heard in public, since one of the Franks Committee's fundamental principles was openness. Most hearings today are held in public although there are a few exceptions, for example where there are considerations of national security, where intimate personal or financial details might be disclosed, or where a medical examination is involved. Openness is a key factor in achieving public confidence and trust in the impartiality of the system.

Legal representation

Prior to the Franks Committee, it was common for tribunals to have a ban on legal representation. Today, there is now only one important tribunal where the ban exists: tribunals appointed to investigate complaints against NHS practitioners. This may well be justified in that it would almost inevitably be the case that a practitioner complained of would take advantage of the right to legal representation and the prospect of being subjected to hostile cross-examination by the lawyer might be off-putting for claimants. There is, however, widespread debate on the question of legal representation. Without it, procedures are simplified, less technical and cheaper, thus reflecting the user-friendly values of the tribunal. Conversely, when legal representation is allowed, procedures become more complex and expensive. This is a pattern which has arisen rapidly in modern tribunals and has led to the judicialisation of procedures in many tribunals dealing with complex issues such as employment and immigration.

Legal aid

Legal aid is a closely related issue to the right of legal representation. Under the current law, legal aid is not available for legal representation before tribunals, with the exception of the Lands Tribunal for Scotland and the Employment Appeal Tribunal. Otherwise, a party who qualifies can receive advice under the statutory scheme ABWOR (Advice By Way of Representation). This normally involves advice being given before the hearing. However, the legal adviser is entitled to go into the tribunal and advise a client as long as they remain silent (otherwise it would be a fraud on the legal aid scheme). The Franks Committee recommended that legal aid should be ultimately extended to all tribunals, however, to date, this has not been achieved. The concept of extending legal aid has also been frequently highlighted by the Council on Tribunals. In 1973, the Lord Chancellor set up a committee to consider extension to all statutory tribunals, but ultimately rejected the idea.

Yet, the issue of legal aid and representation continues to be important. Research in the former Supplementary Benefit Appeal Tribunals showed a 30 per cent success rate for represented claimants, as opposed to 6 per cent for unrepresented ones. Similar statistics can be found before other tribunals and seriously place doubt upon the usefulness of the current system. But critics continue to argue that the introduction of legal aid will result in lawyers becoming commonplace in the tribunal system, leading to ever-increasing formality. They also recognise that lawyers do not always possess the necessary expertise for certain tribunals, such as the Mental Health Review Tribunals, and that non-lawyers with relevant experience are often more skilled. Furthermore, tribunal work is not popular or financially attractive, and there may be a tendency for young, inexperienced lawyers to appear, who are not as experienced as some non-lawyers.

Inquisitorial

Tribunal procedures are intended to be run on an inquisitorial basis, ie the chairman can call and examine witnesses himself. The advantages of this are that it keeps costs down and maintains an air of informality. It also redresses the imbalance in that a relevant government department will be represented by an official who is an expert in the branch of the law in question, and so has an advantage over an unrepresented claimant, or even a solicitor.

Giving of reasons

Another key recommendation of the Franks Committee was that full reasons should always be given for any decision. This reflects the principles of natural justice and is embodied within the right to a fair hearing – *audi alteram partem*. A decision is apt to be better if the reasons have to be set out in writing, since it is more likely to be better thought out. Also, if there is to be an appeal, then a reasoned decision is essential in order that an appellant can assess the grounds for appeal. The duty to give reasons was implemented by the Tribunals and Inquiries Act 1958 and is now contained in s 10 of the 1992 Act, which provides that it is the duty of a tribunal to furnish a statement, either written or oral, of the reasons for a decision. The only grounds for refusal to give reasons are where it would be contrary to the interests of national security, or contrary to the interests of the individual concerned. Some tribunals may also be exempted by the Lord Chancellor or the Lord Advocate from the duty to give reasons, but the Council on Tribunals must be consulted first on any such proposal.

A useful authority on giving reasons can be found in *Re Poyser & Mills' Arbitration* (1963) where an arbiter failed to give adequate reasons to an agricultural tenant concerning a notice to quit which had been served by his landlord. Megaw J said that the duty to give reasons must be read as meaning that proper, adequate reasons must be given. They must also be intelligible and deal with the substantial points that have been raised.

Expenses

The courts principle, ie that an unsuccessful party pays the other's expenses, does not apply to tribunals, even where the hearing is between two private parties. The only exception can be found in the Scottish and English Lands Tribunals. The Franks Committee also considered that a successful party should be given a reasonable allowance to cover travel, subsistence and attendance of witnesses. Some tribunals, but by no means all, now have such discretionary powers.

APPEALS FROM A TRIBUNAL

Appeals from tribunals differ according to the governing legislation for each one. There are no hard and fast rules as to the routes of appeal, however, many statutes convey a right of appeal to the sheriff court and thence to the Inner House of the Court of Session. Where a right of appeal is given to a sheriff and the statute gives no indication about review of the sheriff's decision then it is presumed that the sheriff's decision is final. However, in almost all cases there is a right of appeal on a point of law to the Court of Session. Sometimes there is an appeal on fact or law to a higher tribunal, and usually from there to the Court of Session. Where there is no appeal, there is the possibility of judicial review.

The appeals system has been much criticised since it has no real consistency for citizens and reflects the refusal of the legal profession to accept the separation of tribunals from the ordinary courts. The Franks Committee considered the suggestion of creating an Administrative Appeal Tribunal which would be distinctly separate from the ordinary courts. However, this idea was rejected for a number of reasons, including the fact that a body of law might build up which would conflict with the ordinary law, and that such a body would need unsustainable levels of staff to cope with its wide jurisdiction. On the other hand, Franks did think that there should always be a right of appeal to a higher tribunal before going to the courts, such as the relationship between employment tribunals and the Employment Appeal Tribunal. This recommendation has not been universally applied.

REFORM

In May 2000, Sir Andrew Leggat was appointed to undertake a fundamental review of the tribunal system in the UK. His report, *Tribunals for Users: One System, One Service*, was published in August 2001 and was highly critical of the current system. Leggat felt that tribunals had developed in an *ad hoc* manner, had inadequate appeal procedures, and generally had no real independence. In order to deal with these issues, he felt that tribunals should be brought together into a single system with a common administrative service and a clear appeals procedure.

Government response to Leggat was at first slow, however, in July 2004 the Department for Constitutional Affairs (DCA) published a White Paper, *Transforming Public Services: Complaints, Redress and Tribunals*. This paper sought views on the Leggat proposals and has led to the draft Courts and Tribunals Bill. At the time of writing, the Bill is still being prepared for introduction to Parliament, however, it is likely to contain a number of important innovations. It is intended that most existing tribunals will be unified under a single body known as the Tribunals Service which will provide common administrative support. This non-statutory body has already been set up within the DCA in anticipation of the new legislation. It has responsibility for 16 of the largest tribunals including the Employment Tribunals Service, and the Appeals Service, with more to be added by 2008.

The Bill will also introduce a simplified two-tier structure for tribunals. A lower tier will consist of tribunals hearing appeals as normal while an upper tier, in the form of an Administrative Appeal Tribunal, will be established to deal with appeals against decisions from the lower tier. There will also be a right of appeal via statutory review from the upper tier to a single Court of Appeal judge.

It is intended that the draft Courts and Tribunals Bill will be presented to Parliament during 2006, with reform taking place on a staged basis until April 2009. It is expected that the scope of the Bill will only extend to non-devolved, central government tribunals, although many of these have a UK-wide jurisdiction and thus the provisions will also have some effect in Scotland and Wales.

PUBLIC INQUIRIES

Overview

It is common for statutes to lay down that a public inquiry should be held before a particular decision is made. This may commonly occur when there is a question of government policy affecting the rights of citizens, such as the building of a new motorway, or the location of a land-fill site. Holding a public inquiry allows the communities affected by such actions to voice their concerns over issues such as disruption and environmental impact. There are many thousands of inquiries held in the UK each year, and they arise from specific statutes as well as the Tribunals and Inquiries Act 1992. The number of specific statutes providing for the holding of inquiries is vast and include areas such as company affairs, railway disasters, salmon fisheries and bridge tolls. By far the most common relate to the use of land, especially proposals by public bodies compulsorily to purchase land, or proposals under the Town and Country Planning Acts.

Procedure and operation

Despite serving a variety of purposes, inquiries tend to follow a generally universal procedure. The Minister involved in a decision will appoint a Reporter (called an Inspector in England) to conduct an inquiry into particular matters. He or she will hear the parties in proceedings similar to those of the ordinary courts, and will report back to the Minister, who will then take the decision. That is the traditional position, but in some cases the decision-making is delegated to the Reporter.

It is important to note that an inquiry is merely one step in the administrative process leading to a policy decision. While the inquiry will help the decision-maker to decide what is best in the public interest, he or she is not confined to the material presented at the inquiry, unlike a court, where the decision is based on what is said in court. Other factors, such as government policy, may ultimately influence the decision. For example, with a proposal to build a land-fill site evidence may be produced that it will be environmentally detrimental for the local community. But the Minister is not confined to that evidence, since he or she is entitled to look at wider issues, and may decide to allow the proposal on other public policy grounds, for example the creation of jobs.

The starting point for considering modern procedures must be the Franks Committee on Administrative Tribunals and Inquiries (1957). At the time of the Committee, there was widespread concern and dissatisfaction about the way public inquiries were conducted. The official view was that inquiries were purely administrative and that government departments were obsessed with secrecy. Objectors had no right to know the reasons for the proposal to which they were objecting and reasons were not always given for decisions. For example, in *Local Government Board v Arlidge* (1915), Hampstead Borough Council made a closing order under statutory powers in respect of a house deemed unfit for human habitation, and it subsequently refused an application to determine the order. The respondent appealed, and the Board appointed an inspector to hold a public local inquiry. The inspector took evidence and visited the house, but eventually confirmed the closing order. It was held that the appellant was not entitled to see the report made by the Board's inspector on the inquiry.

The Franks Committee sought to remedy the faults of the system of public inquiries and concentrated on seeking procedures which would balance the conflicting interests of those involved. The Committee recommended that, as with tribunals, procedures should be guided by the general principles of openness, fairness and impartiality, but, in the case of impartiality, should be subject to qualification since government policy might be involved. In particular, Franks recommended that:

(1) the individual should know in good time the case he would have to meet;

(2) any relevant lines of policy laid down by the Minister should be disclosed at the inquiry;

(3) an independent inspectorate should be set up;

(4) the inspector's report should be published along with the letter from the Minister announcing the final decision;

(5) the decision letter should contain full reasons for the decision; and

(6) it should be possible to challenge the decision in the courts on the grounds of jurisdiction and procedure.

In 1958, the Government took action to bring most of these recommendations into force (apart from the independent inspectorate) and in 1959 it acquired statutory power to make regulations about inquiries. These are now contained in s 9 of the 1992 Act which gives such power to the Lord Chancellor (or the Lord Advocate in Scotland). There has subsequently been a flurry of procedural rules, such as the Town and Country Planning (Inquiry Procedures) (Scotland) Rules 1964, and the Compulsory Purchase by Public Authorities (Inquiry Procedures) (Scotland) Rules 1976. Inquiries have also been brought under the supervision of the Council on Tribunals, which has to be consulted about procedural rules by the Lord Chancellor in England, or the Lord Advocate in Scotland.

The Court of Session and the English High Court have contributed to a further understanding of the statutory rules surrounding inquiries and have been prepared to infer, from the general statutory context, the need to observe the rules of natural justice, insofar as they are not inconsistent with the statutory provisions. In recent times, the courts have tended simply to say that proceedings must be "fair" rather than use the legalistic overtones of the phrase "natural justice". In *Lithgow v Secretary of State for Scotland* (1973), Lord Dunpark said: "Even if there is a set statutory procedure, it is not enough for the decision-maker to comply with it: he must exercise all his powers fairly in relation to those who object to fair exercise. He must always give all parties the opportunity of adequately stating their case."

So a party must be given a fair opportunity to put their case, and answer all significant points adverse to it. If the Minister or Reporter proposes to take into account any factual information obtained "behind the back" or after the close of an inquiry, it must be disclosed and opportunity for comment must be given. In *Hamilton v Secretary of State for Scotland* (1972) the Secretary of State confirmed a compulsory purchase order after an inquiry was held. The objectors claimed that the case had been altered without their having an opportunity to meet it. It was held that the Secretary of State was acting in a quasi-judicial and not an administrative capacity in confirming the order, and therefore he should not act contrary to the rules of natural justice

What fairness demands in any particular case depends on the nature of the subject-matter and is to be judged in the light of practical realities as to the way administrative decisions are reached. But the courts will take a broad view and will not concern themselves with the observance of technicalities more appropriate to a private issue decided by a judge.

Tribunals of Inquiry (Evidence) Act 1921

A specialised type of inquiry is that which Parliament can authorise at any time under the Tribunals of Inquiry (Evidence) Act 1921. This has no particular connection with administrative powers, or with administrative law for that matter; for though it has been used to investigate allegations of administrative misdeeds by Ministers of the Crown, civil servants, local authorities or the police, it is not confined to such matters. This kind of inquiry is one of last resort and should be used when nothing else will satisfy public disquiet. It will usually centre around sensational allegations, rumours or disasters. There have been some 20 such occasions when this type of inquiry has been used, including cases of improper gifts to Ministers, a leak of information about bank rates, disorders in Northern Ireland and the Aberfan landslide disaster involving the National Coal Board. It should be noted that this type of inquiry is very much an exceptional event.

ESSENTIAL FACTS

- Tribunals are bodies which are distinctly separate from the court structure, and are independent of government departments. They can be either statutory or non-statutory but most are set up by statute and their powers and scope are contained either within the statute or in regulations issued under its authority.
- Tribunals have a limited scope of authority to deal with administrative-type issues, which are often, but not necessarily, disputes between public authorities and citizens.
- The modern tribunal system was shaped by the recommendations of the Franks Committee (*Report of the Committee on Administrative Tribunals and Inquiries* (1957)) now consolidated in the Tribunals and Inquiries Act 1992.
- Tribunals should be open, fair and impartial, meaning that they should be free from government interference, have clear and consistent procedures, and should be held publicly, giving clear and reasoned decisions.
- The key advantages of tribunals are speed, cheapness, accessibility, informality, expertise and flexibility.
- Legal aid is unavailable for tribunals except the Lands Tribunal for Scotland and the Employment Appeal Tribunal.
- Tribunal proceedings are subject to the principles of natural justice and their decisions may be subject to appeal or review.
- Public inquiries are afforded by statute and commonly occur when there is a question of government policy affecting the rights of citizens, such as the building of a new motorway or the location of a land-fill site.
- The modern public inquiry system was shaped by the recommendations of the Franks Committee (*Report of the Committee on Administrative Tribunals and Inquiries* (1957)) now consolidated in the Tribunals and Inquiries Act 1992.
- Inquiries are subject to the principles of natural justice and should be conducted fairly.
- Tribunals and public inquiries are scrutinised by the Council on Tribunals which is a statutory body with a consultative and advisory role relating to the constitution and operation of tribunals and inquiries.

INDEX

access to courts, denial of, 38
actio popularis, 50
Acts of Parliament
  Scottish Parliament, of, 3, 31–33
  UK Parliament, of, 3, 11–14
ad vitam aut culpam, 7, 10
administrative law
  definition of, 1
  history of, 1–2
  Scotland, in, 2–3
affirmative parliamentary procedure,
  29
appointment of judges, 10
audi alteram partem, 65

background, 1–3
bias, rule against, 66–68
byelaws, 33–34

central government
  departments of, 19–20
  generally, 19
  non-departmental public bodies, 20–21
  structure of, 19
collective responsibility, 15
commencement order, 26
concluded view, forming a, 67
control, separation of powers and
  executive and judiciary, 6–7
  judiciary and legislature, 7
Council on Tribunals, 91–92
cross-examination, 70

declarator, 61
delegation, improper, 54–55
delegatus non potest delegare, 27, 54
"devolution issues", 32
devolved government
  generally, 21–22
  Scottish Parliament, 21–22
discretion, fettering, 55–56
doctrines of the constitution
  independence of judiciary, 9–11
  ministerial responsibility, 15–16
  rule of law, 14–15
  separation of powers, 5–9
  sovereignty of Parliament, 11–14

error of law, 52–53
evidence "behind the back", 69
executive
  judiciary, and
    control and, 6–7
    exercise of functions, 7
    membership overlap with, 6
  legislature and
    exercise of functions, 7
    membership overlap with, 5–6
exercise of functions
  executive
    judiciary and, 7
    legislature and, 7
  judiciary and legislature, 7

fair hearing, right to, 68–73
"fairly incidental" rule, 39–40
fettering discretion, 55–56
First Minister, appointment of, 22–23

"*gouvernement des juges*", 57

"Henry VIII" clauses, 7, 26

illegality, as ground of judicial review
  delegation, improper, 54–55
  error of law, 52–53
  factors in, 53–54
  fettering discretion, 55–56
  generally, 51–52
  purpose, improper, 54
impartiality of judges, 11
improper delegation, 54–55
improper purpose, 54
independence of judiciary, 9–11
individual responsibility of Ministers,
  15–16
indivisible authorities, 68
inquiries *see* public inquiries
interdict, 61–62
irrationality, 56–58

Joint Committee on Statutory
  Instruments, 29
judges
  see also judiciary

judges (*cont.*)
  appointment of, 10
  impartiality of, 11
  privilege, legal, and, 11
  removal of, 10–11
judicial privilege, 11
judicial review
  generally, 47
  grounds of challenge, 51–59
  remedies in, 60–62
  scope of, 47–49
  title and interest to sue, 49–50
judiciary
  executive and
    control and, 6–7
    exercise of functions and, 7
    membership overlap with, 6
  independence of, 9–11
  legislature and
    control and, 7
    exercise of functions, 7
    membership overlap with, 6

law
  error of, 52–53
  rule of, 14–15
legal aid, in tribunals and inquiries,
  94–95
legislature
  executive and
    exercise of functions, 7
    membership overlap with, 5–6
  judiciary and
    control and, 7
    exercise of functions, 7
    membership overlap with, 6
legitimate expectation, 72–73
local government
  borrowing powers in, 41–42
  powers of, 23, 40–42
  structure of, 23
  ultra vires doctrine and, 40–41
Lord Chancellor, separation of powers
  and, 8

maladministration, concept of, 86
membership overlap
  judiciary
    executive and, 6
    legislature and, 6
  legislature and executive, 5–6
  local authorities, in, 67–68
ministerial policy, 68

Ministers
  responsibility of
    collective, 15
    individual, 15–16

natural justice, 65
NDPBs *see* **Non-departmental public
  bodies**
negative parliamentary procedure,
  29
nemo iudex in causa sua, 65
Next Steps Agencies, 20
**Non-departmental public bodies
  (NDPBs)**
  accountability of, 21
  generally, 20–21
notice
  prior, 69
  reasonable, 69

ombudsman
  see also **Parliamentary Commissioner
    for Administration; Scottish Public
    Services Ombudsman**
  generally, 77
  meaning of, 77
openness, 93

Parliament, sovereignty of, 11–14
**Parliamentary Commissioner for
  Administration**
  appointment of, 78
  complaints to, 79–80
  enforcement by, 81
  introduction, 77–78
  investigations by, 80
  jurisdiction of, 78–79, 87
  reform of, 81–82, 86–87
  reports by, 80–81
  tenure of, 78
participation, 67
pecuniary interest, 66–67
presumptions
  access to courts, denial of, against,
    38
  liberties, interference with, against,
    38–39
  non-retroactivity of subordinate
    legislation, 38
  sub-delegation, against, 39
  taxation, against, 37–38
privilege, judicial, 11
procedural impropriety, 57–59

procedure
public inquiries, in, 98–100
tribunals, in, 93
proportionality, 56–58
public inquiries
operation of, 98–100
overview of, 97–98
procedure in, 98–100
purpose, improper, 54

quangos, 20–21

reasons, giving of
administrative decisions, in, 71–72
tribunals, at, 95
reduction, 60
remedies in judicial review
declarator, 61
generally, 60
interdict, 61–62
reduction, 60
statutory, 62
removal of judges, 10–11
representation, legal
administrative process, in, 70–71
tribunals, in, 94
"reserved" areas of legislation, 31
retaining model of devolution, 22
rule of law, 14–15

Scottish Executive, 22–23
Scottish Parliament
Acts of, 31–33
background to, 21–22
composition of, 22–23
legislative competence of, 31–32
powers and functions of, 22
subordinate legislation of, 33
taxation powers of, 22
ultra vires doctrine and, 22, 31, 33
Scottish Public Services Ombudsman
appointment of, 82–83
complaints to, 84
enforcement by, 85
introduction, 82
investigations by, 84–85
jurisdiction of, 83–84, 87
reform of, 86
reports by, 85
tenure of, 82–83
separation of powers
generally, 5

separation of powers (*cont.*)
control, in
executive and judiciary, 6–7
judiciary and legislature, 7
exercise of functions and
executive and judiciary, 7
executive and legislature, 7
judiciary and legislature, 7
Lord Chancellor and, 8
membership, overlap in
judiciary and executive, 6
judiciary and legislature, 6
legislature and executive, 5–6
Supreme Court and, 8–9
sovereignty of Parliament
generally, 11–12
legal basis for, 12
limitations on, 13–14
statutory instruments
challenge in courts, 30–31
committees, examination by, 29–30
consultation of interests on, 28–29
controls on, 28–31
generally, 28
Joint Committee on, 29
parliamentary controls on, 29
publicity and, 30
Standing Committees on, 30
ultra vires, 30–31
sub-delegation, presumption against, 39
subordinate legislation
generally, 25
justifications for, 25–26
legality of, 26–27
non-retroactivity of, 27, 38
Scottish Parliament, of, 33
statutory instruments, 28–31
Supreme Court, 8–9

taxation
powers of Scottish Parliament, 22
presumption against, 37–38
tribunals
appeals from, 96
constitution of, 92–96
Council on Tribunals, 91–92
expenses at, 95–96
generally, 89
legal aid for, 94–95
openness in, 93
procedure at, 93
reform of, 96–97

tribunals (*cont.*)
representation, legal, at, 94
using, reasons for, 90–91
***ultra vires* doctrine**
general competence, power of, 42–44
generally, 37

***ultra vires* doctrine** (*cont.*)
local government and, 23, 40–44
omission, by, 44
presumptions surrounding, 37–39
Scottish Parliament and, 22, 31, 33
statutory instruments, 30–31